How?

Daniel M. Lewis

Copyright © 2017 Daniel M. Lewis

All rights reserved.

ISBN-10: 1545424330
ISBN-13: 978-1545424339

Attention: Quantity discounts for book purchases are available to your company or educational institution, for reselling or educational purposes, subscription incentives, gifts, fundraiser campaigns etc.

For more information please contact
info@DanielSpeaks.ca

DEDICATION

I dedicate this book to my beloved family who has stood by my side through all the ups and downs and in-betweens. My mother and father; Selvin and Marie Lewis, My beloved wife and best friend Renata. Jonathan, Natalie and children, you are irreplaceable in my heart.

I wrote this book as a loving husband, and upon completion I have now become a loving father to special boy, Jacob Samuel Lewis. May this book serve as a testimony of God's love, and proof that;

"Our setbacks in life, only propel us farther ahead"
– Pastor Selvin Lewis

Daniel M. Lewis

CONTENTS

	Acknowledgments	I
1	OMG!	Pg #1
2	How?	Pg #3
3	Valentine's Day	Pg #5
4	Sand Box	Pg #12
5	The Race	Pg #19
6	First Concept	Pg #25
7	That's A Rap!	Pg #29
8	The Record	Pg #46
9	Early Graduation	Pg #54
10	Man Of Steel…Toed Boots	Pg #64
11	Job's, Job's, Job's!	Pg #76
12	The Last Nail	Pg #84
13	Cut	Pg #89
14	Renata	Pg #103
15	I Promise	Pg #113
16	Knock-Knock (The Domino Effect)	Pg #120
17	I Do	Pg #127

18	Sacrifice	Pg #134
19	The Apple Tree	Pg #146
20	T	Pg #158
21	T "Bye-Bye" Daniel	Pg #166
22	Bricks	Pg #176
23	The Beginning	Pg #186
24	Me	Pg #196

ACKNOWLEDGMENTS

I believe everyone has their own unique story, but it often takes people that believe your story is worth telling, to encourage you to share it.
This book would never be written without the passionate support and hard work of my lovely wife Renata Lewis. Thank you so much for the long nights of conversation about this book and the silent tea dates of rigorous editing.

A special thank you to my father and mother; Selvin and Marie Lewis for always reassuring me that I can do anything I put my mind to. Thank you to all the people named in this book, whether friend or foe, you helped to create my story and shape my views about life. I have no regrets. Special thank you to Chanele McFarlane from Vision Vertical for your thorough edits and uplifting feedback. There are so many other people that I can thank, but I'm certain you already know who you are.

Thank you to my Lord and Saviour Jesus Christ for saving me and showing me hope where there was no hope. Without you I would be dead and forgotten, but you protected me and gave me a voice and a smile forever.
I promise to use these tools to bring you glory.

OMG!

OMG!

Is this really happening? Am I really seeing this?

Am I actually looking at hundreds of people screaming and running for their lives at the Toronto Zoo while being chased by an over-sized bird? I know what you're thinking, "He's got to be kidding!" I wish I was, but unfortunately, I'm not. It looked like something out of a scene from a classic episode of The Road Runner gone terribly wrong. I mean, there were a few men at the zoo that day that perhaps forgot to shave for a few days, but none of which I can truly say resembled the Wild Coyote. So why was this happening? A resounding sound began to echo throughout the entire zoo. "*Squeeeeeech!!*" No, that wasn't the ostrich. Ladies and Gentlemen, that sound was me! For a second, it looked like Emperor Ostrich had discovered that someone was hiding in the blue porta potty, like the ones you would see at a construction site. Suddenly, the fear of the oversized bird tipping the unit over with me inside and that rancid unknown stench becoming my newest body wash became intensely frightening. Phew! The echoes of people screaming started sounding further and further away from my bird-proof porta potty hide out. Alas, I was safe. Now, they say people shouldn't judge a book by its cover, but instead by its first chapter. Hopefully, my completely fake and adventurous zoo thriller, which has nothing to do with me, my business, or anything for that matter, has grabbed your attention.

Since you've gotten this far, I'll take that as a yes.

Now, my dear reader, let's get started, shall we?

HOW?

How. How what? What does that mean, and why did you name your book How?
Everybody has a story, and this one is mine.
My life in a nutshell has been a wild 28-year ride. It is loaded with tons of experiences, tons of ups and tons of downs, as you will soon find out.

My story has a tender beginning and winds up taking an incredibly unprecedented turn. Kind of like a good thriller movie (maybe?) There are parts of my life that have always left me in awe, and have left me with one simple question. How? I believe this is not just true to my story. There are probably a hundred things that have left you asking the same question in your life.
There are times in life that whether things work in your favour or not, these make you shake your head in disbelief, and these have been a few of mine.

How did I end up starting my own business after dropping out of high school?
How did I find the money to get my idea off the ground?
How did I end up becoming Brampton's 2014 Young Entrepreneur of The Year without an MBA or any business background at all?
How did our company get nominated as a finalist for 'Best Social Media Reach' in the tea industry at The 2015 World Tea Expo in California?
How did I get featured on Global TV News Toronto and The Globe & Mail?
How did our company have a record-breaking turnout for our store's grand opening in Brampton?
As you can see, life is filled with "hows."

This book also has some tips that have proven to be quite valuable in my business life. If you are an aspiring business owner, you probably want to get to the part of the story where I tell you, "this is how much it costs to start up a business, this is where you go, this is who you talk to and after such and such a time, you'll be stacked with money." Well, not quite.

Right now might be a good time to close this book and pick up one of those "**10 steps to Becoming A Trillionaire in Just 7 Days**" books with the 'Colgate model' on the cover and $100 bills floating in the background. Don't worry about me; I'll wait for you here.
Oh, hey! You're back!
It's been 168 hours and you're still not rich.
Let's pause for a moment of silence.

I'll leave you with a final thought before we jump in. Any powerful book that I have read didn't fill my mind with unrealistic expectations about life. Instead, the most inspiring books I have read are true stories, with true facts that offered me a sense of reality. This book is my reality, and through it I hope you, the reader, can relate to some of the situations, circumstances and outcomes that you see happening with me and other 'boot strapping- grass root entrepreneurs' that started from nothing.

VALENTINE'S DAY

It's February 13 and in most places in North America, couples are preparing to rekindle their love for each other while pouring their hearts out inside colourful Valentine's Day cards. Valentine's Day is the day of binging on chocolate, a day of heart shaped everything, and a time that usually gives men the courage to get down on one knee and pop the big question. How could you not love a day that focuses on love? Is that even possible?

While most people were preparing for this exciting day to come, my parents were already celebrating something special. They were celebrating the birth of their new baby boy.

Now there's an interesting happenstance with this day. Although this chocolate-binging, ring-popping day created the perfect time of the month for me to be born, technically the same song could be sung for my brother, Jonathan. Jonathan was also born on February 13, the day before Valentine's Day. And the most interesting part of this incredible coincidence is that we are not twins. Jonathan was born two years before I was, on the exact same day!

Thanks Jon. Thanks for all the birthday cakes we had to cut in half, all the gifts we had to split, and all the parties we had to share. It has been really special to me. Totally special, totally fair. There, I said it, in the most annoyed yet peaceful voice as possible. (Daniel sighs)

I can imagine that my parents were relieved to finally hold me in their hands, after a long hard fought labour in which doctors said I might not make it. I had somehow managed to completely turn sideways in my mother's womb, making it difficult to pull me out. The doctor brought the most uncomforting news to my dad as he patiently sat in the waiting room waiting to hear my first cry. Instead of hearing "Mr. Lewis, congratulations on your new baby boy!" my dad was asked to sign a document making a choice on whose life should be spared in the event that something went wrong.

Really?

How does a man choose between his wife and his new baby?

I can't even imagine the thoughts and feelings that must have raced through my dad's head at that very moment.

Let's consider.

On one hand is his beloved wife, who together with him will be the unity that builds their future, the person that will walk alongside him throughout life's long journey. They already have a 2-year-old son who's counting on them to be there to raise and nurture him. However, on the other hand, ready to burst into life, awaits a new child. There, in that baby boy, lays an unwritten story waiting for his beginning and hoping for his chance at life.

So what do you do? The doctor needs an answer and time is not your friend.

Boldly, and thankfully, my dad refused to sign the document. He decided not to make a choice, but instead to leave the situation in God's hands. You should know that my dad, who is a strong believer in Jesus Christ, viewed this situation in a spiritual way rather than in a natural way.

HOW?

By choosing either my mother or me, it would be as if he was accepting that one of us wouldn't make it. Faith had taught him that the decision to give life or take life was not in his hands, and certainly not decided by simply inking your name on a piece of paper. From day one it seemed like my destiny was always in God's hands. Thanks, Dad. It has been through the many times my parents have trusted and consulted with God that has taught me to do the same.

You're probably wondering, how on earth does God advise you in life when you don't even see him? You can't just call him up on the phone or send him an email. Through my own experiences, I've learned to look at it this way. When someone needs advice about what's going on within their body, they go to someone that studies the body. That person should more or less be able to give tips, suggestions or solutions on how to maintain your body. In life, I look in the Bible, which is God's Word, to see what He says about various situations that are similar to mine. It doesn't always work the next day, but neither do the prescriptions we get from our doctors. Sure enough, just like my parents, with time and patience, every decision I have made after seeking Godly counsel has always proven to be a good one.

Weighing in at some chubby number, full of hair, and crying uncontrollably, Daniel Lewis was born on February 13th, 1988 at 9:30 pm. I was born in Toronto at Mount Sinai Hospital.

I later learned from my parents that in the Holy Bible, Mount Sinai was a very significant place. It is where Moses who led the children of Israel across the Red Sea, met with God and where God eventually gave him the Ten Commandments. I wonder what my life would turn out to be like? Would I play any major role in history? Better yet, would I get the chance to meet God one day? Sure enough, life has a way of addressing all of our unanswered questions, in time. It may take a lifetime, but eventually, as you travel along your journey, you'll discover all of the "who, what, when, where, why's, and my favorite, the how's." It all seems to unfold, one chapter of life at a time. From my toddler years, I was definitely a mama and daddy's boy. I came to realize who my best friends were from a very early age. No, it wasn't my first friend in kindergarten, or the neighbour's children that I grew up with. My best friend was my dad. My dad was and still is my greatest friend. Since I was old enough to remember, my dad has always taken care of me. My mom is a nurse, and a pretty amazing one at that. It has always been her passion from her youth. She would work very long hours, and spent a lot of my younger years in the hospital assisting all of her patients. I have learned all of my principals and work ethic from her persistent example. She is the hardest working person I know.

At that point I was the youngest child in my family, so you can say I was a little spoiled. When I was three years old, my dad used to always prepare the yummiest breakfast for me, which was usually oatmeal porridge with two slices of bread that I could rip apart and toss into the bowl. I absolutely loved it. He would sit me down on the couch with my purple Flintstones Dino and the rest of my teddy bear collection, and would surf the channels to find the *Barney* show for me to watch as I ate. He would often be doing work around the house so he would tell me to sit there and be a good boy, and I would always listen because he always made me so happy and created an environment for me that was hard for me to leave. My greatest joy was making my parents laugh. So I would always copy them in different ways to tease them. I would tell them all the stories from my babysitter adventures. I would wake up early Sunday morning, dress myself in my best clothes and then take my children's Bible, that I couldn't read yet, and open my parents' door, pretending to read to them and teach them. This is usually what they would wake up to every Sunday. My parents were and continue to be one of

HOW?

my greatest inspirations.

So what's with this spoiled perfect little daddy's boy story? Are you just going to brag about how lucky your parents were to have such wonderful obedient little children?

Well it wasn't all rainbows for my parents. Perhaps I was just balancing the playing field, because my brother had clearly grown to be the troublemaker out of the two of us. Jonathan was the complete opposite of me. He'd rather sleepover at his friend's house, while I preferred to sleep with my parents. He'd rather play sports with the guys, while my excitement came from sharing jokes from my tiny joke book with my mom and my dad. He watched *WWF*, while I watched *Bugs Bunny*. He was a real boy's boy. Rough, loud, and slow to listen. We were worlds apart. Despite our differences, however, I strangely looked up to him. In my little mind, he was almost like a young hero who just knew how to make breaking the rules look cool. My parents were always disciplining him because he was so daring. I would always look on at him, with a pitiful, goody-two-shoes look, as I followed behind my dad and cuddled up to him to show my disapproval for his bad behavior.

One winter afternoon while we were playing outside of our babysitter's house, my brother and his friends decided to put the freshly fallen packing snow to good use by forming smooth snowballs and whipping them at passing cars. I stayed off to the side minding my own business and working away on my snow angel designs, which looked like little fairies on the ground because I was so tiny."Hey you, get over here!"

The sound of screeching tires and some angry guy jumping out of his car in the middle of the road caught my attention. Jonathan and his friends bolted towards the front of the house, and it became obvious that they had hit one of the cars and messed with the wrong guy.

"Dan! Come! Let's go, quick!" My brother yelled.

I quickly abandoned my angel friends and ran as fast as I

could to catch up with Jonathan and his friends. We headed inside the house where Jon and his friends ran upstairs laughing at the mischief they had just done, while I just hung out downstairs saddened by the fact that my snow angels laid in the backyard all alone. Suddenly there was a knock on the door and without any hesitation I answered it. A tall, unhappy man in a dark navy jacket and dark pants looked down at me and asked me if I saw some guys throwing snowballs at cars. Without any hesitation, I pointed towards the stairs signaling that I knew exactly what he was talking about and who the guys were.
Oops.

After our babysitter had come to the door and learned from the gentleman what had just happened, she brought my brother Jon and his friends down to face the man who we had come to discover was actually an undercover police officer.
Oops again.

Something told me that very soon my angel friends were about to become a lot more real to me. Luckily Jon and his friends got off the hook with a simple apology and a warning, but boy oh boy, did I just create some serious enemies. From that day forward, I was banished from ever hanging around my brother and his friends. I couldn't play any of their video games, or play with any of their toys or even look at them for that matter. I was left with no other choice but to spend my days playing with our babysitter's daughter Paula, who kindly took me on as her new companion and playmate in the game of doctor and house.

Overall, my younger childhood years were spent very peacefully to say the least. I learned a lot from Paula about friendship and kindness and even how to create the perfect first date for Barbie and Ken. As I would participate in my daily scenarios of doctor and house, I would always look on with curiosity at my brother and his friends. They were always so loud and competitive and seemed to be having a blast. I secretly wondered if I would ever be accepted again

HOW?

into their group, although my thoughts would then quickly be interrupted with Barbie's latest outfit.

My whole life thus far I had spent with my dad, so naturally as the first day of school dawned on me; I was saddened to say the least. I didn't fully understand the concept of school until the day my dad dropped me off to my first day of kindergarten. The way the school was designed left a gate between my dad and me. He looked at me. I looked at him. And I think it was at that moment I realized he was going to leave me there. A teacher came up beside me and held my hand, motioning to my dad and saying "It's OK, Mr. Lewis. We'll take good care of him."
I thought about our porridge dates. The Barney show.
My joke book. How was I ever going to get through this day without my dad?

As I stood at the gate, my dad told me not to worry, everything was going to be OK and that he would be back for me at noon.
We waved at each other until I couldn't see him anymore.
"Come on Daniel, time to make some new friends", said my new teacher Mrs. Bint.

I looked up at her trusting Kindergarten teacher eyes. Her soft voice and the sounds of other children screaming and playing must have brought some form of comfort to me, because I eventually followed her. And then I saw it.
It was big, beautiful, colourful and full of things to climb... The playground!

SAND BOX

Is a leader born a leader? Or is leadership something that's learned? I don't know if there is a definite answer to this question, as leaders, entrepreneurs and visionaries come in so many different shapes and sizes and operate in so many different ways. I used to hear an old saying that you can always find a leader from inside of the sandbox. Take a walk through a playground one day where there are a lot of children playing and you'll see that the statement actually proves to be correct. In a group of children playing in the sandbox, there is always that one child who gets everyone to form a line or try and build the same castle or even dig a mega ant tunnel. It's amazing to watch because what you're actually seeing is the inception of a leader. Though that child may not know it or be able to identify it, they are able to take charge, bring about structure and give direction to a group of individuals in a very effortless way. Does this mean that they will make a good leader? Not necessarily. You can never tell until the child has grown and matured and carved out their personality and values. These were my "carving years."

From day one in Kindergarten, I learned naturally how to turn the sandbox into the "Dan box." The more children I met, the more outspoken I became. I guess that maybe this sprung from my showman abilities I gained at home from always trying to make my parents laugh. I had developed a love for performing and brought that love to the sandbox. Suddenly the same desire I had to see my parents laugh and smile was translated over to my new friends in Kindergarten. I loved to see people laugh. And I learned to do this in such an infectious way, that the other students would eventually become curious as to what was so amusing over by the "Dan box" and then join the group.

HOW?

As time passed, I learned how to get everyone in the playground's attention, how to play some sports and even how to make the teachers laugh. To top it all off, it seemed that all my time with Barbie paid off. By the first grade I became the mini king of first dates and speaking flattering words to girls, making me the Ken of all Ken's at school. I hung out with all the girls because I knew what they liked, I understood them, and to be quite frank I just loved having lots of girlfriends. Thanks, Paula.

As time went on and my school years progressed, my skills with the young ladies only got better. [Enter problem number one]. When one kid in school is clearly grabbing the attention of all the girls, trouble is sure to follow. Boys, for the most part, are very, very jealous especially when they are young. As I ascended the heights of middle school, rumors spread around my school that one of my female friends' crazy ex-boyfriend from the neighbouring school wanted to fight me, for no apparent reason.
Fight!?
What!?
Wait a minute… Ken doesn't fight!
Remember reader, it's still me. You know, un-confrontational, snow angel making, ratting out troublemakers me. I had never been in any serious fight, and I certainly wasn't going to be fighting anyone anytime soon. At least, that's what I thought.

As I was walking home one day from school with my group of friends, I was approached by a group of guys from the neighbouring school that claimed that they had a problem with me. One guy, whose name was AJ, was obviously the crazy ex-boyfriend, as he stepped into my face and shoved me to the ground. I mustered up some strength and got myself back up, but he pushed me back down. I can't recall exactly how young I was but I was definitely too young to be in any altercation about girls.

After pushing me down continually while my friends looked on, AJ completed his bullying masquerade with a hard, solid punch to my stomach forcing me to the ground and leaving me there screaming and in tears. I got beat up pretty badly. My friends quickly picked me up after AJ and his crew had left and they began their sympathetic ramblings and the millions of reasons why they couldn't help me. I wasn't expecting them to help me because I knew that we were all pretty weak and extremely afraid. Word got around to my older brother Jon pretty quickly that afternoon as he found me in the food court of the nearby shopping mall with my friends grabbing a Toonie Tuesday special from KFC.

He was fuming!

You see, regardless of how siblings may treat each other, at the end of the day, family is family and in Jon's bad boy world, you don't mess with family. The next day after school, Jon was waiting for me by the side door that I usually exited from and he had the same look on his face as the day that I ratted him and his friends out. I slowly walked over to my brother with a few of my friends and he told me to follow him to the neighbouring school and point out the AJ guy that beat me up the day before. I hesitated because I just knew this was not going to be good turnout for AJ. As we walked for a minute or two I spotted AJ just walking out to the pathway that ran along the creek separating the two schools. AJ was with a couple of his friends laughing and walking along with absolutely no care in the world and no clue of what was about to happen to him. For a second, I contemplated not pointing him out to my brother and just pretending that I couldn't find him, but as I thought about that last punch he gave me and how he left me humiliated on the ground, I pointed right at him.

"Are you sure that's him?" Jon asked, for confirmation.

"Yes", I replied.

Then with a loud threatening voice, Jon shouted, "AJ,

HOW?

come here!"

AJ looked around startled and confused wondering who was calling his name out so loud and so anxiously. It took AJ a second or two, but he soon realized who was calling him as he saw my face and my brother beside me walking towards him. What I saw next really changed the course of my life for a very long time. My brother stepped into AJ's face and demanded that he explain why he messed with me, and instantly AJ's tough guy facade shattered to the ground. AJ began to back up pleading to my brother that he didn't hit me -he was just asking me a question. I thought 'OMG! Is AJ actually lying about pushing me around and punching me in my stomach?' Wow! He must be really afraid. After a few seconds of denying and lying, Jon had enough. He punched AJ a good 7 or 8 times knocking him to the ground and kicking him repeatedly until he was in tears, just like I was.

After AJ had reached the point of complete annihilation, my brother stopped, picked up AJ, and looked at me with fire in his eyes and told me to punch him in his stomach.

Uh-Oh!

Are you serious?

I didn't even know how to punch, nor was it in me to actually do it.

At the same time, I didn't want to make my brother any angrier and I hoped maybe after this punch it would all be over and we could just leave AJ alone. After I wrestled with myself on how I would actually carry this out, I clenched my fist and "WHAM!" I knocked him back down to the ground.

Although this sounds like a made up story in an attempt to glorify bullying and fighting, it's not. This was a real incident in my life that was a game changer for me as far as weakness was concerned. I was in for a big surprise if I thought that I was going to make it through this life being super nice to everyone and avoiding fights. Yes, maybe I could do my best to stay away from fighting other people, but what about the fight of life? What about fighting for something I strongly believed in? Would I just fold up, hold my stomach and cry until someone decides to care enough and come to my rescue? No way. I had to be a fighter.

Carving lesson number one from the sandbox: Leaders have to have fight.

I particularly had to be strong because life had a few more AJ's of its own that I was yet to encounter.

Every day of business, and life for that matter, is a fight. The biggest battle is actually starting a business and the most vicious contender is usually ourselves. It's easy to cozy up with a warm cup of tea and plant yourself in the nearest bookstore as you feast away on someone else's success story or road to riches with their groundbreaking business venture, but what about yours?

Many people are unhappy with their nine to five jobs or their corporate careers, but the golden question has been and always will be: What are you going to do about it?

Throughout my life, I was unsuccessful at every idea I tried to build, but as the ideas kept crumbling, my fight to make something work just kept getting stronger and stronger. It's as if I brought my older brother to work to back me up when I needed to get something done. What I gained from this experience was to develop the attitude of a fighter. By no means am I promoting physical fighting, but living a defeated lifestyle is not going to gain you anything either.

In every tough situation I face today, I always ask myself this one question: Did I leave as a loser or did I leave as a fighter? A loser is a person that accepts defeat. A fighter is a person who refuses to be defeated even when they lose. Simply deciding to pick myself up, get stronger and enter the same battle ends up becoming more profitable for me than to sulk about losing for the rest of my life. It is this type of fight, and this type of leadership that has helped me overcome all the obstacles in my life and is the reason why the AJ situations can no longer get the best of me.

Follow the Leader

Throughout middle school I got to learn a lot about myself. As situations face you in life, you grow and your outlook on things starts to change. Although my thoughts on many things had changed, one thing remained the same. I still loved making people laugh.

After many years of performing for my parents, classmates and teachers, I had grown a little older and created my own little philosophy. I realized that entertaining people was not as important as keeping them entertained. People tend to have a short attention span, especially once they lose interest in something that is happening or being said. If I truly wanted to hold on to my class clown title and leader of the pack crown, then I had to keep my 'buzz' buzzing. According to the urban dictionary and a professor at the University of Common Street Slang, buzz is simply a feeling of excitement or a stimulated state of being. It's when something or someone has reached an electrifying peak and it can be felt, heard and enjoyed by all who "catch the buzz." I understood this science very easily in my youth. People liked me, mainly because I would make them laugh, but I began to wonder, What would happen if I didn't make them laugh? Would I still be the coolest guy in the class? So I began to test out my thoughts and the results that I would observe really taught me a lot about being someone that people looked to for leadership. Balance is key, in life, in business, in everything. Being too much of something is never good, and under utilizing your potential can be detrimental as well. It became obvious throughout my school days that people viewed me as a leader, and someone they could look up to and could set the tone for how a situation would play out. Instead of acting like I didn't know that they felt this way, I embraced leadership and purposed in myself to be seen as a well-balanced leader. My thinking was this: If I display a lack of leadership skills, then I'll mislead those who trust me. However, if I overdo it, and start trying to boss people around then I'll actually become more of a dictator than a leader, and we all know that never has a happy ending. My conclusion was to become an unpredictable leader. Sometimes I'll crack some jokes and have everyone in laughter and other times I'll be a lot more quiet and reserved. This wasn't a trick or tactic I was using to mislead or to try to control people. It was the only way I could be a leader without being forced to lead. I still apply this kind of thinking in my business today because it makes leadership enjoyable for me rather than pressuring and burdensome. It helps build me as a strong leader while also leaving room for others around me to exercise their leadership qualities as well. You can depend on me but you don't have to depend on me. I like it that way.

My company T By Daniel has truly benefited from all the lessons I was able to grasp from the days of the sandbox up until I was in my mid teens. I always try to encourage my employees and staff to grab a hold of leadership even in the smallest of tasks that are delegated to them. I may ask one of them to prepare some tea samples and distribute them to patrons walking by our shop, but nothing is stopping them from organizing that task in their own special way and making it their own. They can set up a table outside, grab an instrument, or sing a song. The possibilities are endless, if they can discover their own strengths and keep their 'buzz' buzzing. If they're able to see the value in this kind of liberty on the job, then our customers will continue to be excited about our brand and our employees will continue to grow into strong leaders. I guess this answers the initial question about whether one is born to be a leader or if leadership can be learned. If one is willing to learn it and the teacher is willing to share it, leadership is available to everyone in his or her own special way.

THE RACE

Like a pumpkin at Halloween time, my life was being carved, shaped and sculptured by all the many adventures that I would embark on day to day. Middle school is usually phase two of personality shaping in many children's lives, and for me this is where my athletic abilities were discovered, especially in track and field. I know it sounds easy to just say that I discovered my athletic abilities as a track and field sprinter, but how did it really happen? At what point does someone realize that they can run fast?

In my case, it came in the form of one of my biggest fears. A dog named Rescue. He was a 1ft nothing, feisty Chihuahua with a nonchalant owner walking laps at our local park one sunny afternoon. My dad, who was a professional soccer player in his youth, would often take my brother and I to the park especially to go to the soccer field to kick the ball around and work up a little sweat. He used to be a very well known 100m sprinter back in Jamaica during his college years, so he also had a huge interest in track. As we ran up and down scrimmaging across the field, I suddenly noticed a small, Chihuahua barking and running towards us. For some reason, his owner had let him off his leash to run free. As to why he would do such a villainous thing, I still don't know.

My fear of dogs was intense, and although tiny in size, Rescue didn't strike me as very friendly. This fear of dogs must be genetic as my dad; my brother and I all took off running down the field to escape. To make matters worse, the owner who now saw his dog chasing after three guys, continued walking and laughing at the same time. This angered me all the more, but I couldn't focus on him. All I knew was that I had to keep running! Rescue must have thought we were playing with him but that was far from the truth, because in our world we were running for our lives. My dad saw a way to outsmart the little persistent beast by jumping up and grabbing a hold of the football pole where Rescue was unable to reach him. My brother followed after my dad jumping up and also pulling himself up to safety. Then, there was me. Too short to grab the pole and too scared to stop running, I was forced to exert myself to run as fast as I could. It was clear that nobody was going to "rescue me." *Badum psh*.

I ran, and ran, and ran some more as my dad and brother, hanging, looked on. As I ran, I realized that Rescue wasn't getting any closer to me. In fact I was actually beginning to lose him. And then it hit me. I was fast!

Even with his small little persistent paws gripping the green grass every step he took, my worn out shoes seemed to grip it faster. Eventually Rescue grew tired and decided to return to his owner. Phew! Due to my newfound abilities, I was safe.

During the walk home we all laughed and joked about the Rescue chase and also came to the conclusion that maybe I had what it takes to be a track and field runner. With my dad's experience, he saw that I had what it would take to win a race and encouraged me to strengthen my new skill.

As soon as track and field tryouts were announced at school that year, I was one of the first students to sign up.

When I went to the tryouts, I surprised the coach with my time in the 100m sprints and it became obvious that running was in my blood. As I would set myself up at the starting line, I would remember Rescue and his terrifying little face chasing after me and ZOOM! I was gone.

"Have you seen that fast guy, Daniel, run?"

Word began to spread around the school about my sprinting abilities. With the help of my dad, who became my coach, and a few practice runs, I became the fastest kid in the school.

School track meets were my favourite. The atmosphere was so intense, the competitors were so fierce and the audience was so anxious that it created a feeling in me that I still feel to this day. It was a nervousness mixed with confidence, anxiousness mixed with anticipation. It was such a blend of every emotion and I loved it. It kept me humbly competitive, always striving to win, while also understanding that winning is not a feeling of comfort but instead a reward of extreme effort given. I was a winner, not because I always won, but because I learned how to win.

Track and field became my everything. Everyday I would train with my dad. He would come to all my track meets, and when I wasn't at school he would take me to the park and give me pointers and tips on how to run better. His face in the crowd was my push to always give it my all in every race. I would race anyone who challenged me, and I had many contenders, though no matter how confident they were, they could never take my title of the fastest runner. One of my many contenders, who were as confident as they come, was Chadwin.

My parents moved around a lot throughout my middle school years, so I was always used to being the new kid in school and, having to break the ice again. This was usually done through my jokes, but at Fletcher's Creek

HOW?

Public School, it was done through my speed. As the new kid, you are usually faced with two types of people. There's the friendly kids that can't wait to meet you, show you around the school and find out what you're good at. Then, there's the popular kids. They're the kids who were graced with immense favor to the point where they were so loved and so looked up to that they became just a little cocky. This was Chad. Chad was the king of the school, loaded with boyish good looks, strange humor and apparently endowed with speed.

Now, I had started to make my mark with the students in my grade, racing everyone I could and slowly gaining my crown of speed at this new school. Word must have gotten around to Chad, when one day he suddenly approached me during recess.

"Hey! I'm racing you!"

Chad was the type of guy that would just flat out call you out, and if possible embarrass you and snicker away in his own little strange jokes.

"Alright, sure", I replied. We immediately headed over to the asphalt pathway next to the school where people would usually race. We met at the starting point and someone counted us down.

"On your mark, set, go!"

"ZOOM!" Off we went.

Or shall I say, off I went.

What? Really? This is the fastest guy in the school? It was too easy. He was certainly taller than I was, and was a year older, but neither of these facts served him any good when he was on the track.

I won. He lost. I was officially the fastest guy in the school, once again. As for Chad, well, if you can't beat 'em, join 'em. Chad was an all around sportsman, so he wasn't easily shaken when it came to losing. And this was the beginning of a lifelong friendship.

When my first year of high school came around, I was introduced to a new level of competition and a new roster

of sprinters who were all as hungry as I was.
Everything I learned about competing, I learned on the track.
Perseverance, determination, hard work, fight, willpower, and focus.

All these characteristics were perfected with every stride and every victory that I would attain. My 100m sprinting reputation and flawless record took me all the way through to grade 10, where I finally met my match. I managed to come first in the 100m heat finals at ROPSSAA, which was our school region's athletic association. From there, I advanced on to SOSSAA which was the region representing the entire southern part of Ontario. This is where I faced off against one of my fellow teammates, Antonio. Antonio and I had attended the same school and we were on the same track team. This gave me a sense of comfort because I knew what he was capable of and I had beaten him already in the past. Carving lesson number two: Never underestimate anyone.

What I didn't know is that Antonio had been involved in some intensive training outside of school on his own time, and he came prepared.
"Runners, take your positions."
"On your mark. Set... POW!"
And we were off. All six runners breathing deep and exhaling fast while clawing through the air to gain the lead in the first ten metres. I could hear every runner's coach cheering them on from the side of the track, but only for a second, as we zipped past them reaching the thirty-metre mark. The race was close, and no one was giving up any ground. Everyone refused to fall behind. By the fifty-metre mark, runners had just about reached their top speed and this is typically when the separation starts to occur. As the first two or three runners began to fall behind, I gained more confidence to push for first place.
Then suddenly, I glanced to my right and saw Antonio, but he looked different.

HOW?

He looked calm, almost like he was holding back his true speed the entire race. Suddenly he unleashed the hidden speed he had been perfecting outside of school, and he managed to pull in front of me and win first place in the SOSSAA 100m sprint finals. I was defeated and so shocked that I think I may have even allowed another runner to get ahead of me, putting me in third place. Needless to say I was in disbelief.

When I first founded my tea company T By Daniel, I can't count how many times people would ask me, "How are you going to be better than David's Tea? What makes you better?"

Now for those of you who don't know, David's Tea is a tea chain and leader in the tea industry. Even today, with Starbucks being just a stone's throw away from our retail tea bar, people often ask us, "How are you going to compete with Starbucks?"

My answer is simply to outwork my competition. Exactly like how Antonio did to me. He saw the value in the overtime. He took advantage of the twenty-four hours that were graciously granted to him everyday and with hard work and determination it finally paid off and he advanced onto the top track meet in the province, The OFSAA. And as for me and my track running dreams? Let's just say high school is a very interesting carving period. I eventually hooked up with the wrong crowd and stop going to my track meets. I got kicked off the track team and picked up an interest in music. This carved pumpkin was about to become something or someone completely different. Pumpkin pie, anyone?

FIRST CONCEPT

With track behind me and high school before me, this part of life became a very transitional part of the carving for me. The more friends I made in high school, the further away I would get from my parents. The once fun loving relationship I shared with them started to dwindle, as I began to make my mark with my friends as one of the most popular 'crews' in high school and in our city on a whole. How does a group of teenage boys make their mark in their city?
Simple. Cause a little trouble, of course.

We spent the majority of our time skipping school and would go to the mall because that's where all the good-looking girls from different schools would go in search of food or 'bad guys' like me. In true popular guy style, we would hang out in the dark corners of the food court with our dark shades on. As strange as it sounds, the more we did this, the more well known we became. Girls from all different schools would point us out, and we started to gain a little following. One of our tactics to make us stand out and be easily recognizable was our dress code. In so much that we were dubbed with the name 'BTF' which meant Brampton's Finest. We were flashy; we were trendy and most of the time we were seen wearing our own customized clothes.

I started noticing how impactful clothing could be. What you wore could make you stand out or fade to black. It was an expression of character and had the ability to make you memorable. Thus, though completely opposite from my track skills, fashion became my new hobby of choice. I would always look for clothes that really stood out and reflected my personality. I would take ten-hour bus trips to Pennsylvania to try and find the most exclusive American urban styles, and would come back with luggage bags full of the top name brands of that time. Jackets, hoodies, jerseys, you name it I wanted it and would travel great lengths to get it. When I would go shopping at the local malls, I'd hunt for anything colourful, anything bright, and anything that was one-of-a-kind. But Canadian malls were very different from the American malls. The variety was limited and the price points were much higher. It became increasingly difficult to find clothes that would fit my newfound style and passion for fashion.

With every problem comes a solution, and I decided to take matters into my own hands. I began designing my own clothing. I teamed up with my good friend Tay who was very skilled at drawing. Tay was my neighbour and the type of guy who, if you saw him, you would never think would be interested in something like drawing. I guess that's why you should never judge a book by its cover. He was tall, muscular and looked more like he could pursue pro wrestling rather than the arts. Tay was the popular of the populars. The young ladies loved him, and the young men, well… not so much. So aside from his artistic skills, Tay was a seasoned 'fighter' who had to learn how to defend himself from all his haters. He had won his fair share of fights in high school and became one of those guys that very few people would ever try to mess with. When it came to the arts, Tay was especially talented in airbrushing and would create these really cool templates of random things like flames, icebergs or even famous cartoon characters. He would then trace them onto t-shirts, sweaters and jackets and we would both sit there for hours and hand paint several pieces of clothing. Finally I was able to wear the type of clothes that I was comfortable in. The type of clothes I would find in the States. The greatest thing about it all was that it was totally unique, and it had all the kids at school intrigued. People started asking us where we got our clothes and when we told them that we made them, my first business venture began. Ironically enough, we decided to call our new clothing line 'First Concept'. It became an adventure, rather than a venture and to be totally honest I had no clue what I was doing in terms of the business aspect, but I enjoyed every minute of figuring it out. With Tay's amazing artistic skills and my outgoing personality, the word of our custom clothing line started to spread. We began designing shoes, boots, headbands, wristbands, car interiors and pretty much anything that we could draw on or apply fabric glue to. If I was to calculate how long it took us to complete one of our designer pieces and divide that time by how much we eventually sold it for, we were probably making -$45/hr. Skipping math class only made matters worse, but the point is we did it because we loved to do it.

The apparent success of First Concept managed to turn the head of my heroic big brother. So Jonathan also got caught in the fashion wave and decided to start his own clothing line with one of his friends. His creative juices must have been really lacking as he decided to call his clothing company "Second Elements."

OK fine, we have the same birthday, but really, Jon? A clothing company?

Named Second Elements?

Luckily throughout middle school and high school, I had regained my status from the snow angel days and Jon and I became pretty close. Despite our rocky childhood beginnings, we've always maintained a great relationship. If he decides to do something, chances are I'm going to do it too, and vice versa.

Ladies and gentlemen, this was the beginning of my very first entrepreneurial experience. It was small, unorganized, and motivated by impressing high school girls. But it was driven by passion and fueled by adventure and curiosity. Above all, I didn't even know that this was considered an entrepreneurial venture. I didn't even know what an entrepreneur was. Carving lesson number three: if you find something you love to do, you will never feel like you are working.

As most teenagers, though I enjoyed my fashion clothing line, without any discipline or structure, my clothing line eventually kind of just vanished. *Vamoosh*! Gone! Like it never even happened. But the desire to do something different was still there. I was usually trying to apply myself to something creative, occupying my free time with the next big idea. Though technically my free time wasn't really free. I was still skipping school and my school grades were suffering. I wasn't the worst kid in school. I respected my teachers as much as I could, and most of my teachers enjoyed having me in their class, as I would still try to make them laugh. My problem was I really had a hard time focusing in class. I was distracted by thoughts of the mall after school, my friends, and what I was going to pursue next.

Outside of school, however, was a bit of a different story.

The world was changing and so was I. My desire to continue to fulfill the passion that I once found in First Concept was still bubbling in me. Cellphones and gadgets became a big deal, which meant borrowing twenties from my parents, or doing the Pennysaver route in my neighbourhood could no longer sustain my latest needs. My unquenchable need for the most updated looks in fashion continued to grow. And then there was the rise and influence of rap music.

Anyone got a mic?

THAT'S A RAP!

Rap music was everywhere, and quickly became the most popular genre of music in the early 2000's, or at least that's when my innocent ears began to listen to explicit lyrics (behind my parents back, of course).

From Jay-Z to Eminem, 50 Cent to 2Pac, it was clear that rap was the future. Rap stars were glorified on TV in a way that was hard to ignore. They wore the best clothes, were always seen with the prettiest girls and drove the most expensive cars. In my teenage mind, this was legendary.

So, being naturally fond of entertaining others, I developed a skill for writing rap songs. I would write and practice and then write and practice again until I actually became really good with words and coming up with punch lines on the spot. I guess practice does make perfect, or as my dad would put it, practice makes permanent. Finally, a new skill. A new way to entertain, and a new way to make people laugh. I loved it!

The ability to rap and rhyme on the spot is better known in the rap world as freestyling. Every time I would freestyle, crowds would quickly formulate and the "ooohs followed by the 'ahhhs' and the 'Woooo's' would start to attract more and more people to the crowd. Someone

would drop a beat and the rest was magic.
"If you're looking for the Cap-tain then I'm it, like a cheese cake on fire, I'm the Pie-lit"
"You can see my pencil yawning, because it's so tired, of Robin William people - who like to 'Doubt Fire"
"Now do you make that list? Go ahead and take your pick, I think if failure was religion I'd be atheist."

Every time I heard a beat, I was in my zone, and the words would just come. Sort of like my track and field days, once that beat started, I just kept going.

As usual, Jonathan was inspired by my latest venture, and decided to take a shot at rapping as well. To our surprise he wasn't that bad. At this point my brother had grown alot since the days of throwing snowballs, and his bad boy persona matured into what people would call 'swag'. He was so comfortable in his own skin. He was strong, and he was confident, and even if he wasn't the greatest at something, that never stopped him from giving it his best shot.

A couple of my other friends took a shot at the whole rap trend and in grade 10 my second venture was formed. I'd rather leave out the gory details of what the corny name we came up with for our group was, but I will tell you the story about how I got my personal rapper name.

One day, while I was doing my thing, freestyling for the high school crowds, someone in the mob shouted out and said "Honestly, D's Nice! "What he was actually saying was "Daniel is Nice." And that was that! I dropped the 'I' off 'nice' and made it a 'y' to give it a bit of an edge and my first stage name became 'D-Nyce'. The name was simple but effective. It was short, but catchy and most importantly it was real to me and to those who heard me. The name involved me, while also leaving enough room for someone to wonder "Who's D? And what is he nice at? So there I was. A 15-year-old boy now in a rap group. Rapping was great, I felt so cool and fulfilled, but there was still something seriously lacking in my life. Can you guess? I'll give you a hint... Cha-ching!

If you guessed money, you got it. Remember how I told you all about how I couldn't live off the Pennysaver route anymore? Well at this point it couldn't have been truer. An aspiring rapper definitely needs more than $40.00 a month. So I did what every kid my age would have done. I spiffed up my resume and walked right on down to McDonald's. When they called me for an interview, I put on my best classic attire, practiced interview questions with my parents, and off I went. After answering all the questions and doing my best to charm the interviewer, I landed my first real job. I started off as a lobby cleaner, picking up all the left over garbage on tables and making sure the seating area was clean. I did it with all my might, because remember I had dreams and these dreams needed money. As my managers watched me work they admired my work ethic. I applied everything I saw at home, especially from my mom, at McDonald's. I was always early for my shifts; I would stay later if they needed extra help. I would pick up my co-workers' shifts and I always made sure my uniform was neat and tidy. No wonder my mom was always so busy. Her work ethic made her stand out, and eventually it made me stand out. They began to train me on cash, and in no time I was serving customers behind the counter- my first real experience in customer service. I applied all of my skills I had discovered thus far. I tried my best to lead when the possibility arose and to follow when I was being instructed. I would try my best to make each and every customer happy and make their time at our restaurant special. So, in just over a year of hard work and dedication, I was promoted to a shift manager. This was fantastic! As a manager I was able to take all the shifts I wanted to make more money. I got experience motivating a team. But the greatest thing about being a manager... was that I got to hire people. Want to take a guess at who my first hire was?

Was it Chad? Or maybe Jonathan? Or what about the

HOW?

airbrushing bad boy Tay?
How about all three!
Life was magic. We would dance and sing for customers, freestyle in the back room, and at this point we were all making money. As the money rolled in and the stability of our jobs were pretty solid, we realized that every serious rap group needs a manager. He had to be clever, a good talker, smooth, and willing to take on a challenge. He had to be good as a team player, and yet, not a rapper.
Now, not everyone in our little crew was a skilled freestyler. But the worst would probably have been Tay. He just didn't have the rapper flow. He would try, but it wasn't his thing. However, Tay was definitely a ladies' man, and somehow we thought that would be beneficial to our success. Don't ask. We just decided he was the perfect person to represent us. So *BANG*! Tay became our first manager.

Throughout high school, our names started buzzing now more than ever before. With athleticism and First Concept behind us, we had already gained traction and popularity. Now we had money, so we could afford to buy the latest styles, purchase a recording microphone to make our own songs…and get this. We even bought our own cars!

Girls loved us because we were like a local boy band sensation. It was pretty cool I must admit, but with every lover comes a hater. That's where things began to get ugly.
Haters. They started popping up everywhere, all the time. These were mostly guys who we grew up with and sometimes they were even complete strangers at parties who for whatever reason didn't appreciate our hustle. The interesting thing about a hater is that most of the time they don't even know why they hate you, they just do. Ever go on a celebrity's page and read the posts under their pictures? The majority of comments are strong words full of hatred from people who have no idea who they are talking about or why they are full of so much hatred

towards that person. It is truly a sad reality.
My friends and I quickly went from BTF (Brampton's Finest) to BMH (Brampton's Most Hated) and we were pretty much hated by every guy who wasn't in our little group. It started with basement parties after work, where guys would challenge us to a dance off. They would dance. We would dance. We would win, and they would hate us all the more. Then there was freestyle battling. Again, they would rap, I would rap, and I would win. I'm not suggesting that I was better than them. Perhaps it may just have simply been my genuine passion or the days I spent practicing, but I was known to never back down and I never lost a freestyle battle.
If it wasn't freestyling then it was some guy who had a chip on his shoulder because his ex-girlfriend was dating one of my friends. There is always a reason to hate someone who is trying to follow his or her dreams.

Rumors began to spread around town about us on popular online platforms like MSN, and people would call us the Brampton F*g*ts. It really sucked.
Although at times difficult to avoid, my parents always taught my brother and I that fighting never solves anything and that it takes a bigger man with a stronger character to just walk away from an altercation.
Didn't your parents say the exact same thing?

According to a study conducted by the University of 'Come On Let's Get Serious', research shows that 99% of young teenage boys who are faced with other teenage boys trying to humiliate them, especially in front of teenage girls, will most certainly lead to an altercation. Let the fighting begin. But first, allow me to quickly interject. Reader, please know that I am firmly one hundred percent against bullying, fighting and any unnecessary altercation that leads to another human being, being mentally or physically hurt. Of course it is much easier for me to stand by my words as a twenty-seven year old, (when writing this chapter.)

HOW?

But we're talking about me at seventeen.

I always tried my best to follow my parents' advice. As much as I have always hated fighting and altercations, I had learned to defend myself very well when necessary. But this was not the route I wanted to take. I was still a lover, not a fighter. So I crafted new ways of fighting and defending myself against these haters, in hopes that it wouldn't lead to anything unnecessary. Yeah, right.

So, do you think you know me well enough yet to guess my weapon of choice? If you guessed music, please give yourself a pat on the back. Music became my battle arm. It was a bit out of my nature to make music directed at a group or a person to bring them down. So my life took a pretty dramatic turn as I began to use alcohol as liquid ammo to constantly reload my lethal weapon of words. You see, physical fighting is quick and unpredictable. In a scuffle, there are no definite factors that promise one person will be able to defeat the other. It doesn't matter if you're bigger or smaller or tougher or more experienced, all it takes is a simple slip up and your opponent can floor you in a second. This was far too complex for me. However, I discovered that words on the other hand had a much bigger impact. Words can be distributed quickly or slowly, they can confront someone head on or they can indirectly attack someone. With words I was able to think, target and attack the haters in a way that I found effortless and others found entertaining. Instead of just making songs about dreams and aspirations of becoming successful, now I was making what was called 'diss tracks.' Diss tracks were simple freestyles and songs with no choruses, no hooks, and no structure. Just a beat and a few minutes to release your hot displeasure towards someone else.

At this point you're probably thinking, is this book called *How* or *8 Mile*?

In all seriousness though, things were getting bad. I started getting more known for my diss tracks against people than my positive songs. The more tracks I would release, the more scuffles we would get into. Many haters started recording songs towards us and a miniature version of the Jay-Z and Nas feud was reincarnated.

One day, when we were all hanging out at the mall as we usually would, a fight broke out with a few guys we knew that went terribly wrong, for them. We were all scuffling, when suddenly the mall security guards jumped out of nowhere and tried to catch us and break us apart. Both groups took a run for it, but one of the guys that we were fighting dropped his cell phone in the commotion and it was quickly picked up by one of my friends. It was a bad call, literally, and the beginning of a much more severe feud.

A few days had passed since the altercation at the mall and in my world it was all forgotten. I thought that maybe, like a soda can, when you shake it up, it gets all fizzy and ready to explode. But if you leave it alone for a little while, it eventually settles and calms right back down to its normal state. I was terribly wrong.
At this point I was still a beloved manager at McDonald's, and our location had become a very popular hang out spot in our area. I had been at McDonald's for a few years and most of the customers knew me by name. Looking back, it felt pretty cool to be so well known. But you know the old saying that I just made up, "well-known, means easily located! Especially by the people that hate you."

One night as I was finishing my shift, I was standing up in the lobby area chatting to a couple of girls that I knew from school. As I stood there casually talking I noticed about six guys dressed in dark shirts and hooded sweaters, that were mischievously approaching the front door of the restaurant. At first I thought, just a regular group of troublemakers stopping to grab some chicken nuggets before they go out to cause some havoc. But as I continued to observe, I knew something was very wrong when two of the guys remained outside of the restaurant

HOW?

blocking the door so that nobody could come in or leave. I left the conversation with the girls to get a better feel of what was happening. As I started to become aware of what was formulating in front of me, another four guys came into the restaurant from the back exit taking the same formation and barricading the doors. I made eye contact with one of them to see if maybe I could recognize them. Great.

I did. It was the guys from the silly mall altercation and by the looks of it they were back for their friend's cell phone. Now luckily, there were not a lot of people in the restaurant at the time, but the few that were there looked very worried about what they were seeing unfold.

One of the guys from the group approached me with a calm yet sinister look on his face and said,

"So, where's the cell phone?"

Before I continue to explain how this all went down, I want you to pause for a second and jump into my mind at this moment...

I'm standing in my workplace of which I am the manager. Ten random guys just came into the store dressed in dark clothing and barricaded the doors. One of them just approached me, confirming that they were there for me. I am also surrounded by customers and my teammates who have terrified and clueless looks on their faces about what is actually going on. How am I going to rap my way out of this one? Was I scared? Surprisingly, no. At least not yet. From my track and field days, I somehow taught myself to overcome fear. Through my experiences thus far, I learned that fear itself was actually afraid of people who knew that being fearful was a choice. Was I worried? Extremely! What was about to happen? What are the customers thinking right now? Are the customers and team members safe? Am I even safe? Am I going to lose my job? So let's push play.

"What phone? I didn't take anyone's phone." I replied facetiously.

BOOM!
That is the sound of someone's anger flaring up after hearing an answer they didn't want to hear. He immediately shoved me and I almost simultaneously answered back with a fist to his face. Being the unskilled fighter that I am, I didn't realize that when throwing a punch and clenching your fist you should not tuck your thumb under your fingers.

So...*Crack*!

No, that wasn't his face breaking under the mighty power of my strength. That was the sound of my thumb breaking from throwing a terrible punch. Before I could even fully realize my thumb was broken, black shirts and bandanas surrounded me, as a gang of guys jumped on top of me throwing punches and kicks and knees and elbows. I tried my best to remain tight, shielding my body from all the blows while trying to push the crowd away from me, but I was unsuccessful.

THUMP!

Suddenly it was silent. All I could see was black. This black, however, wasn't hoodies and bandanas anymore. It was a more peaceful and comforting darkness. I faintly began to realize that my eyes were actually closed. I heard faint whispers and tiny voices and felt soft hands all over me. The voices got louder and louder and clearer as my head began to rise. I must have blinked a hundred times before I actually opened my eyes and when I did, two concerned paramedics held me gently with one holding my head and the other trying to see if I had regained consciousness. About twenty people encircled me as I started to come back to myself and realize what had just happened. The paramedics began to explain to me that I was involved in a pretty serious fight where I had been struck on the head with an iron crow bar and the suspects had taken off. They then explained to me that my parents had been called and asked me if I wanted the ambulance to take me to the hospital. At this point I could never guess how deep in trouble I actually was, and I didn't want to run and hide at the hospital. Remember that little inspiring quote I said about how fear is afraid of the fearless. That quickly went down the drain. Fear set in at the moment and felt very real. The only thing was that I didn't know who to be afraid of. Should I have been afraid of the guys who did this to me? Or of the police who are going to want to question me? Should I have been afraid of my employer? Or of my parents? I was confused and afraid, and my head was really starting to hurt.

Business Lesson from a Teenage Rapper

Life is loaded with crazy curveballs. Whoever thought that the boy who just loved to make people laugh, would end up being the teenager on the floor at McDonald's that was just brutally attacked by a mob of guys looking for their stolen cellphone. But that is the key. Understanding that life, and in particular, business has unexpected twists and turns, makes it easier to bounce back and keep pushing.

Now I don't just want to simply tell you my story. My goal is to also show you about the unexpected events in life that actually taught me a lot about business. Little things that I did as a child or as a teenager actually proved to be worthwhile in building my business, if I just opened my eyes to see it that way. So, without further adieu, let's begin with lesson one:

The Name
My favourite place to be at in business planning. Naming a business. I think the most exciting moment of my "rapping" stint was when I finally found the perfect rapper name to suit me. Remember that little story I told you about D-Nyce?

D-Nyce remained my rapper name for the remainder of my musical endeavours. It was a name that stuck. It was easy to remember. It was cool, and overall, I felt that D-

Nyce represented me. It represented my style and the mark that I wanted to make.

In business, there is a great similarity. I don't think there is anything more exciting than dreaming about starting a business, and then finally finding a name for it. You may be at the startup stages just brainstorming potential names for your company, or maybe you're thinking about rebranding and changing your current name. But the naming of anything, whether your business, your child or your next rap album, is flat out FUN.

A name is a very defining thing. It provides a conclusion to the jumbled thoughts of the mind. Think about naming a child. You have all these ideas of what you think would sound cute. You look up definitions, and you even say them out loud to see how it would sound. But when the baby comes and you seal his or her name, it's over. All your thoughts come to a calm. You stop researching meanings and stop changing your mind. The focus then becomes all about raising this baby and making sure that everything is in place for the new addition to the family. Likewise, the name of a business is very crucial and really contributes to the general success of the business. Once you settle the name, you can move forward into registering that business and get the wheels of its operations turning. However, the naming process can take some time and here are a few things that I have learned. If the name isn't easy to say, then people won't say it. If the name is too long, then people will often misspell or mispronounce it. This can be detrimental to your business over time, as the wrong information will end up on the internet, social media and even text messages when people are discussing you.

As a customer to many different companies myself, the name of a company means a lot to me. I tend to be more loyal to the companies that have trendy, fun, creative names, because they resonate with my personality. I actually feel like they made the business with people like

HOW?

me in mind. This creates a personal touch for me as the consumer and thus, strengthens my commitment to the company. Names carry value. Yes, it's true! There are cheap names and there are expensive names in every industry. This does not mean that it will cost more money to register a certain business name over another. The value aspect that I'm referring to is embodied in the laws of perception. Perception is the way we understand things, the way we regard things using our senses. It's actually our mental impression about something or someone. Names happen to be a huge factor in our decision making in any scenario.

Let's use a jewelry store, for example. One jewelry store is called 'Diamonds For Less' and another jewelry store is called 5th Street Diamond Co. This example is a no brainer. It's terribly obvious which name sounds more valuable. "Diamonds For Less" gives off the impression that their merchandise is much cheaper than any other jewelers around. Whether this is true or not, the store name can immediately give a sense of lesser quality merchandise, just because of the name.

'5th Street Diamond Co.', on the other hand, sounds like an expensive diamond boutique in a popular shopping area in the city. One might feel more confident purchasing their merchandise here, as the name sounds more prestigious and expensive. Not many people would want to tell their friends that they just purchased their wedding ring at 'Diamonds For Less.' Would you? Whether your answer is yes or no, it's truly amazing what a name can do! When naming your business make sure it's accurate to the image you are trying to give to your customers.

So, want another pointer to know if you chose a good name for your business? Here's a simple test. Find a nickname for it and see how that sounds. A good business name should easily create a nickname.

My "rapper" stage name started out as D-Nyce, but over time, after I became well known in my community and throughout the city, there was no longer a need for the 'D'. Instead, everyone started calling me 'Nyce.' I liked it! It had a nice ring to it, and it was rather self-explanatory in my opinion. The take away point here is the fact that there could be many different variations of my name, but all in all it didn't confuse anyone or sound terrible. It was just... Nyce.

McDonald's became Mickey D's. Tim Horton's became Timmy's and Starbucks Coffee became Starbucks. These are all perfect examples of name variations that stand the test of time, even when used as a nickname.

Yes, yes, yes! I know you're very anxious to get those business cards printed and in circulation, but to do that, you'll need a name. Start brainstorming, or perhaps you might want to start freestyling?

Lesson number two:

The Message

All over the world, everyday of our lives, in every mall, every car, every club, every restaurant, every religious sanctuary, everywhere, we listen to music. Everyone has their select few music artists that they love to sit back, relax and listen to. It's very safe to say that we are all serenaded by words and actions that complement our beliefs and ideologies.

But why?

Why do we listen to the music that we listen to? Why do we become fans of certain music artists over another? Why do we embrace one and disdain another? The answer is simple.

It's the message!

Musicians, bands and artists alike, are all judged by their message. What is the artist saying? What is the artist doing? Where are they going? Why are they going there? What is the artist promoting or coming against? These are the key questions we subconsciously ask ourselves when we listen to a song or watch a music artist perform. If the message speaks in favor of what we believe, we support the artist. If the message speaks against what we believe, the artist falls into our ignore/dislike pile, never to be heard again.

As a former rap artist, my message wasn't really different than any other young aspiring rap artist. I would rap about money (that I didn't have), about driving expensive cars, girls, loyalty to my group of friends, dislike for my enemies and the music hustle. Pretty cliché huh?
Now you're probably wondering, what was so "Nyce" about my message? Well to be honest, it wasn't really nice. The reason why anyone would even take interest in what I was rapping about is because of how I delivered my message. The message is very important, but the delivery can easily determine how the message is received. A company's message doesn't only consist of what the owner says it is. It's interpreted in every aspect of the business, from company name, the tagline, the slogan, the jingle, the color scheme, the website, and pretty much everything that has to do with that enterprise!

Whether I understood this at the time or not, I would naturally practice on perfecting and reinventing the delivery of my message. I would rap fast using words in a puzzling way that challenges and forces the listener to unravel and comprehend my lyrics. I would sing certain songs and attach a catchy hook to create a smoother vibe for certain songs. I would use a numerous amount of metaphors and figures of speech to get my message across in a more creative and abstract way. I started to pronounce words using an exaggerated, sarcastic voice to add character and personality to my lyrics. I genre-hopped into pop and rock and R&B. I wore costumes with spikes on my wrist and a long black wig. Yes, a wig.
I tried everything, without any boundaries.
If I had to consolidate the message of my artistry into one word, it was "limitless."
Everything I would do and sing about promoted living life

without any limits. My thinking was, I have nothing to lose, because, well, at sixteen and seventeen I actually really didn't have anything to lose. At least that's what I thought.
It didn't matter who didn't like me, because I strongly believed in my message. If someone didn't think I was good enough, I wouldn't stop getting better. I would beat that pen and paper until my talent became undeniable. I believed the only way I could ever fail, was if I stopped, and I wouldn't stop. I believed, one can never discover who they are until they've explored who they can be.
There were no borders. There were no walls. There were no barriers. I was limitless, and my delivery of this belief was the same.

I have generally always stuck by this message. After all, limiting yourself in any way, leaves you wondering if you ever really did give anything your all. My message as a rapper created this 'limitless' way of thinking, and although my message changed when I entered into the world of business, the 'limitless' frame of mind remained the same.
Lesson number three:

The Haters
In business and in life it is very likely that as you start up or continue to grow you will have individuals, companies and competitors that behave very similar to the haters I described from my rap days. It could be for the silliest reasons.
They think your company name sounds like theirs.
You supposedly copied their logo.
People envy your hunger to succeed.
Your products look the same or taste the same.
Or maybe you're just the newest player in your industry and the more established companies don't like competition. Whatever the case may be, it is inevitable that these situations will arise. In the early stages of starting up T By Daniel, I remember feeling like a certain competitor was copying my ideas. I would come out with a tea

product and a month or two later they would come out with the same name, same product description or same concept with their own little spin on it. It was frustrating, to say the least. The most annoying part about all of this is that the company had started first and was much further ahead than mine, so my complaining ended up looking like I was just jealous of their success and perhaps I was actually copying them. Despite my continual efforts of trying to establish my own brand and find creative ways of differentiating myself, it was useless because they were always the originator in everyone else's eyes. If I was anything like the old me, I would have probably written the greatest 'diss track' in history.

Along the way, I've learned that competition is actually very healthy and it keeps you on your feet. The moment you start a business and begin to carve out your name in society and experience some degree of success, give it about ten months and you will have a direct competitor breathing down your back. Guaranteed!

How will you react to this competition? What if their product is better than yours? What if they have more start up capital to innovate and initiate ideas more effectively than you can? Will you close up your shop or become bitter and start bashing your competition with negative PR articles and ads? Or will you use *bizdom*?

Bizdom is a word I just made up by combining business and wisdom. Let me tell you something, there is definitely some *bizdom* in watching what your competition is doing. However, there's a saying that says, "If you try growing your business while continually looking over your shoulder at what your competition is doing, then you will always be reactive instead of proactive." Imagine running your business that way, only reacting to what your competition is doing instead of looking ahead for future opportunities to become an innovative trendsetter or leader. If watching your competition is the only way you can figure out the next move for your business, then you're probably better off joining your competition and working for them. "If you can't beat 'em join 'em!" You know the old saying.

In business, when your competitors knock you down, use real *bizdom* and become resourceful. A resourceful person is someone who can quickly find clever ways to overcome difficulties. This is how I had to learn to push myself especially during the early days of T By Daniel. I thought of creative things that I was willing to do that perhaps my competitors were not, or maybe couldn't do, based on their message. In other words instead of reacting to them, I wanted to make my competitors react to me. That's when I hit the studio and started recording tea anthems and songs and dressing up in costumes to promote our products, and these are the different little things, which have helped differentiate me from the rest, which I still do to this day. Outwork your competitors, out-service your competitors, out-innovate your competitors, but in all you do, refrain from revenge. Revenge is one of the worst motivations known to man in every way. I wish I would have known this when I was younger.

THE RECORD

Weeks had gone by since the altercation at McDonald's and once again there was a false sense of calmness in the air between my friends and the guys who attacked me. It felt like a hurricane had passed by and now we were in the eye of the storm. Everything seemed normal, the sun was shining bright, but I knew that at any moment the ferocious winds of fury would soon return. We were ready to revenge. Giving some time for things to cool off was very beneficial for my friends and me, as time allowed me to disappear from the radar of the police involved in the investigation of what happened that night at McDonalds. It also gave my employer time to believe me, that I wasn't the Hansel and Gretel of trouble, leaving bread crumbs of disaster behind me as I came to work, and it also gave our new archenemies time to believe that we had moved on from the altercation. Eventually though, my enthusiasm for work began to disappear, and the desire to succeed in music and impress my friends was stronger than my desire to make Big Mac's. So after missing shifts and making too many mistakes to name, I was eventually let go from McDonald's.

  Now, remember when my friend took one of the

haters' cell phones after it had dropped in the mall fight? Well, that phone turned into gold in our hands as we plotted our vengeance. We looked through the phone like any other curious phone finder would and we were able to retrieve some important numbers just incase we would ever need them. Our plan to revenge was crafty, risky and if properly initiated would ensure that the guys who attacked me with the iron crow bar would definitely know that they messed with the wrong guy. The plan was carried out over a two-week span. It was sheer genius. I started calling one of the guys pretending to be a girl who got his number from a friend of a friend. I had a pretty amazing ability to do voice imitations and disguise my voice like a male or female upon command. I guess being forced to play the mom in house can have its benefits. Thanks again, Paula. I enhanced this skill by necessity, as I always had to disguise my voice like a girl in order to call my girlfriends who weren't allowed to talk to boys on the phone when I was younger. After years of doing this and many, many girlfriends, let's just say I kind of mastered the voice-over scheme.

    I called the haters a few times a week just to talk and touch base to create a very realistic scenario. It was actually working, and they really started to believe I was some gorgeous girl from a different high school who had a lot of girlfriends that loved to have a good time. I pried on the fact that I knew these guys. I had information about them, like what they do and who they know, and although they were suspicious at first, clearly their desperation mixed with their curiosity led them to believe that I was really a girl that liked them and wanted to get better acquainted.
One night I called one of the guys and explained to him that my parents would be going away for a few days and the house would be left alone to me. I continued to tell him that I would be having one of my best friends over and asked if he'd like to come over with one of his friends. Got him! Anxious and vulnerable, he thought this was his

HOW?

big break and he quickly agreed. I then begged him not to invite all of his friends, as I didn't want my parents house to get trashed on account of some big surprise house party, and I seasoned this lie by telling him that I had nosy neighbours. And so, the blind date was set and the haters were our confirmed guests.

My friends and I set up a random street to meet on and instructed the guys to come to a random house number where I supposedly lived. Meanwhile, we were all patiently waiting in bushes and at the sides of houses to make the surprise attack on the two desperate haters. We were so young and dumb, that we didn't even consider that maybe while we were walking around the neighbourhood at night with logs and bricks and baseball bats in our hands, that maybe, just maybe someone in the neighbourhood might spot us. But when I thought of the pain and embarrassment that these guys caused me with that surprise attack at my workplace, I was all the more ready to carry out this vicious plan. It had certainly gotten easier to imagine myself throwing a punch, compared to the last time I was left humiliated as a kid by AJ, the middle school bully.

Finally we were all in place and up the street I could see two guys walking, coming towards the house. Their excited disposition on their way to meet two girls who have the house to themselves was a clear giveaway that these were our targets. They came closer and closer until the point where I could almost make out their conversation. My blood began to boil and my heart started beating faster. My hands got extremely tense, as I held on to my piece of wood ready to pounce on them.
"GET THEM!" I yelled!
A fleet of young teenage boys jumped out of their hiding places and began to attack.

I was never brought up around violence. I've never seen any aggravation or abuse from my parents. I was raised around joy and laughter and family and fun and this was what I always displayed to my peers. Love, happiness, joy and friendship.

Wow. Who have I become and what happened to the real Daniel? Even in the midst of revenge, as I leaped out of the bush to attack the guys who assaulted me with an iron crow bar, something in me held me back from actually connecting a full blow with my wooden log. Deep inside I only wanted to scare them; I didn't really want to hurt them. I just wanted them to know that they didn't get away with what they did to me. My friends on the other hand threw bricks and punches as we attacked the two guys who had managed to break free from our grasp and take a run for it. Some of us chased them on foot, while me and a couple of my friends ran to our cars in attempt to catch them a little quicker. We threw our weapons in the back seat of my car, which was actually registered under my mom's name, and zipped down the street chasing after the two guys cutting through front lawns and running through backyards. As I ripped down the street I blew past a black mini van with two men sitting in it and it felt like slow motion the way I saw their faces stare me down as I drove by. Immediately the black mini van swung a U-turn and raced behind me with blue and red lights flashing.

Uh-oh! Why was this black minivan so intent on following me? Want to take a guess?

Well, if you guessed undercover cop in a minivan- *DING DING DING*! You win. And as for me? I lose.

BUSTED! My life was over. Even so, there is no way I'm going to pull a high-speed chase through the streets of Brampton. I was bad, but not that bad. Suddenly three police vehicles both marked and unmarked with officers screaming *"get out of the car with your hands up in the air"* surrounded my car. Their guns were drawn, and this wasn't a new stage in the video game San Andreas or some Hollywood action flick. This was very real. We quickly yet cautiously stepped out of the car with our hands up high and the looks of a sincere surrender on our faces in hopes that the officers would perceive that we were just some young fools who found themselves in a very stupid situation. We showed no resistance, so the cops respectively handcuffed us and put us in their vehicles. It must have been about an hour later that I saw a tow truck arrive and begin hooking up my car. My car as I mentioned happened to be registered in my mom's name. Once again, do you recall that intelligent proverb I enlightened you with earlier about fear and how I don't believe in it? Forget that. My mom was going to kill me!

The cops brought us back to the police station and drove into an underground garage where the entire fleet of cop cars park. From there they took us out of the cars and guided us through an entrance door into an elevator leading up to a room with a desk and chair and I sat there and waited forever. Finally an officer came and asked me some questions about the incident, had me sign some documents and then led me to another room. This room was gloomy, grey and cold and all I could see was steel bars and one open cell with a metal bed and a stained, steel toilet.

Go figure. I think I'm in jail. While I was being guided to the open cell that awaited me, I noticed many other cells with two or three guys in them just sitting around or sleeping, and some were standing with their arms hanging out of a cell and their heads down. This was the lowest part of my life thus far, and I still wasn't sure how I actually ended up here. I remember one officer came into the jail hallway with two McDonald's Happy Meals in his hand and opened one of the cell doors about two down from mine and handed the meals to the inmates. I thought to myself, I bet you I know which McDonald's they just came from. This was nothing like what I had seen on TV about cops and how cruel they are to prisoners. These cops seemed to have a relationship with some of the inmates so it was pretty refreshing to see. Luckily there was no one in my cell, and I came to learn that young offenders don't share cells.

"Nyce, are you in here?" A voice yelled out from a few cells away.

"Yeah, I'm here! Are you good?" I answered back. It was Tay. Tay had also gotten arrested that night. Suddenly, I felt a very slight comfort. At least I wasn't completely alone, and if worse came to worst and some crazy fight broke out in the jail like how you see in those movies, I had the strongest friend I knew just a few cells down with me. We began conversing in friendship code and making light of the situation pretending to be proud of what we had just done. Another one of my friends was also in one of the cells, and the feeling of isolation began to disappear. We talked, we laughed and I even started freestyling as one of my friends provided an echoing beat that bounced of the cell walls. Things weren't as bad as I thought, at least for a little while.

Four hours passed and the smiles had vanished, the cell became ice cold and fatigue began to set in. I turned into my cell and I was faced with a half eaten bagel and an open carton of milk that sat on top of the toilet. It looked like it had been there for years, but the bagel had no mold on it so I knew it couldn't be that old. Either way I felt nauseous just looking at it. I sat down on the cold steel bench or bed or whatever it was and started replaying the incident back in my head. Hours went by, no blankets, no talking, no meals, just me, and my deep thoughts. I was afraid to think about how long I would actually have to stay in here, so I clouded my mind with other thoughts like my past girlfriends and lyrics to some of my songs.

So this is what it's like to be locked up in jail. You can only move in your mind, and even that kind of movement has limitations when you think about what you did to land in jail. Could I ever recover from this low place? How will I ever be a normal person again in the eyes of society? Why didn't I just pay attention in school and get good grades so I could become a doctor or

HOW?

something like every other kid I used to make fun of. I thought of my dad, and my mom, and how disappointed they would be to hear the news of where I was. I also remembered what they would do in difficult situations. So I prayed. I knew God was probably not very impressed with me either, but still, in my heart I asked if He could somehow get me out of this mess, and I promised that if He did, I would never end up back here again. I'm supposed to know better than this. I came from a decent family, raised on Christian values ever since I was born. However, knowing what's right and doing what's right are two completely different things. I wished that I had listened to my parents.

After what felt like a day had gone by, I heard keys jingling as an officer came towards my cell. Unfortunately, the officer had no Happy Meals in his hands so once again my heart sank. The officer began unlocking the cell as I sat there like a sad puppy whose owner had just come home. He told me to get up and follow him and I hoped this meant I didn't have to come back to the cell. He brought me into an office and then explained to me that my dad was here to bail me out. It looked like my prayers were answered. I was free! I signed some more documents and then the officer handed me my shoes and clothes in a large zip lock bag and told me I was free to go. As I approached the main foyer I saw my dad. The man that was my best friend. The person who I always wanted to be around and impress, there he was. He looked right in my eyes. The expression on his face wasn't angry and it definitely wasn't happy either. In disappointment his eyes seemed to ask "How?" How could you do this? How could you end up here? Where did we go wrong?

As soon as I came to him he turned and thanked the officers and proceeded to exit the station heading to the car parked outside. I was so nervous as my dad was completely silent. There was an unspoken understanding that right now was not the time to talk. I didn't know what to say and neither did he. Do I apologize? Should I explain what happened? As soon as my lips went to form words, I couldn't muster up the courage to actually say anything. The ride home was the most violently piercing silence I had ever experienced. Once home, he opened the door, put his keys down and went upstairs to his room. My mom was home as well, but she remained upstairs, and didn't say a word to me. For the first time ever, I felt divided from my true best friends. I had become a different Daniel, and clearly my parents did not approve.

I was charged with assault with a harmful weapon, mischief and masking disguise with intent. Perfect. A great addition to add to my credentials. Seventeen years old, jobless, and now young offender with a criminal record.
Can everyone just sigh with me for a moment?
I tried so hard all my life to make it in the music industry and I could have never imagined that my first actual 'record' would have played out like this.

EARLY GRADUATION

I often wonder how despite all of those recent experiences I shared with you; I still managed to make it through to grade twelve. My attendance was certainly not even close to good but surprisingly, despite my behavior I knew that school was still something I couldn't completely give up on. I guess maybe in the back of my mind I thought that I would be able to balance it all, my dreams, my friends, my work life and school. Unfortunately there were no freestyling courses at St. Augustine Secondary School and the teacher's tolerance for the class clown could only sustain you for so long. I don't think that any teacher ever really wanted to fail me, but my marks would always give the final verdict. My lack of focus, mixed with no studying, and no real genuine ambition to be an academic scholar had a long-term effect on my destiny forever.

So there I was. I had miraculously managed to stumble into grade 12. It was a regular chilly afternoon. I know it was chilly because I can recall wearing my washed out navy blue school sweater and grey school pants. I would never be so properly uniformed if it wasn't cold. Remember how Will Smith used to wear his school blazer inside out with the floral pattern design showing on *The*

Fresh Prince of Bel-Air? That was me, always trying to make my mark in fashion. It was about 1:00pm and I found myself walking across the football field with one of those things on my back that has a bunch of zippers. Apparently it's supposed to hold pencils and binders and things of that sort.

Now if you know anything about high school, you would know that school does not finish at 1:00pm. So what was I doing? Where was I going? I would soon be forced to answer this question for myself.

It finally happened. I actually got kicked out of school. Or maybe I dropped out. As much as this moment in life stung, as I walked across the field alone, I couldn't say that I didn't see it coming.

So how did it actually go down?

Well… it went a little something like this.

I was in my English class. My teacher, lets just call her Mrs. Jones, in case she ends up reading this book, had assigned us to read a suspenseful novel called *Shattering Glass* by author Gail Giles. For the past few weeks the class had been discussing the book, debating the issues in the storyline, and searching for the deeper messages that the author had tried to communicate.

Now I should also mention to you that to this poor teacher's detriment, Chad was also in the same class. As you may have guessed, we were infamously known for interrupting lessons with silly jokes, bursting out into laughter and distracting other students. Mrs. Jones typically had a good tolerance for us, but I guess she was just not into it that day.

Back to *Shattering Glass*. Now, without getting too much into the details of the book, there was this character, a frog, that basically symbolized some deep feel-good meaning in the story plot. Mrs. Jones posed a question to the class:

"In the novel *Shattering Glass*, what does the frog symbolize?" Noticing that no one else was raising their

HOW?

hand, Chad saw this as the perfect opportunity.
With a big goofy smile and giggles ready to burst out, Chad shouted,
"Hoppi-ness! The frog...he symbolizes hoppi-ness!"
And that was it.

My high school education came to an abrupt end as I burst into laughter. It was a loud, tear-filled uncontrollable laughter. The kind where you wish you could stop and control yourself, but you just can't.
I laughed. She yelled. I cried. She screamed. I hit the floor, and if I didn't leave the portable at that point, I'm certain she would have probably hit me if she could.
I did the whole office drill, called my parents, and signed the suspension notice. As I walked away from the office to start heading home, I realized in myself that it didn't make sense anymore. Obviously, this is not the ideal place for me to be. It's not really benefiting me. It's certainly not benefiting my teachers and it's causing distractions to my fellow classmates. So after deep consideration, I decided I wasn't going back to school anymore.
So Daniel, what was the reason you dropped out of high school again? Getting a criminal record? A crazy rap star dream? Making diss tracks in the hallways and getting into fights? Nope! It was just that darn hoppi frog. Thanks Chad. Life was turning out just fabulously for me.

Sometimes we find ourselves stuck in the cycle of life. I'm certainly not suggesting that anyone drop out of school. But what about that nine to five dead end job that isn't really benefiting you, your family or your employer? What about that "I thought I loved it" career that you're still holding on to, when really you'd rather be teaching people how to shape pottery or make jewelry, or take photographs. You see it's hard to actually come to terms with yourself sometimes and make the necessary changes to further your life ahead. Like me, you're probably sitting in that super-serious 'bored meeting' (pardon the pun) bursting into laughter inside. Maybe even tears. Maybe the innovative "creative bug" is biting you. But day after day, you continue to fight and hold onto something that you're really not sure you even need.

Leaving high school was not a failure. It was simply my early graduation. Immediately I started to graduate from people like Mrs. Jones, who honestly didn't think I had what it took to become anything good in life, whether I laughed out loud or not. I began to graduate from society's status quo that says, "If you don't have a diploma/degree you'll never get a proper job or career." I actually began to graduate from myself. I started thinking differently. The only difference with my graduation from a normal graduation was that, there was no cheerful music, no photo ops, no speeches, no hugging, no tears and certainly no tossing the square hat in the air.

Is it going to take a "Hoppi Frog" for you to make the move into entrepreneurship, or make that next step in your career, or make that defining move in your life?

Or would you rather carry on as is? That's your call.

Today, whenever I'm asked to speak and share my story with students, youth or any other audience, I always try my best not to discourage them from the school route, or that successful entrepreneurship does not mean you must quit everything cold turkey and focus on starting a business. That's simply not true. However, it is the reality for many entrepreneurs such as myself.

Graduation is a celebration of completion, advancement and achievement, and that's exactly how I felt at that very moment when I decided not to go back to school. I wasn't sure what I was going to do when I got home, and I certainly didn't have a clue of what I would be doing when I woke up the next morning, but I still felt like I was advancing. It's a weird theory because anyone in their right mind would ask, "How can you advance by dropping out of school?" Well, think of it kind of like a failed relationship between two people. Although they're separating and leaving something that they once held dear

HOW?

to them, they can at least look forward to the new opportunities that await them. They learned a lot and hopefully they can apply these lessons to better their lives. This was me looking forward.

Since we're on the school topic, you're probably wondering "How were your grades Mr. Too Cool for School? Maybe you didn't finish high school, but certainly you were an A+ student... right? That's got to be it! That's how you knew exactly what to do when you landed in the world of business! Wrong.

When it came to my grades in school I never saw many A's on my tests or report cards, in fact C's were the most common grade for me. I always remember bringing my report card home to show my parents and every single time they would look it over, they automatically pointed all their attention to the comments or the notes about me. How was I in class? What are some of the actual observations that the teacher is noticing about me? These were most important to my parents because it showed them who I really was when in a class setting. They compared the teacher's notes to their own knowledge about me at home and from there, they could tell if I was being consistent in the behavior that I displayed at home or if I was a shrewd student who knew how to play the fence. Whether the teacher's review about me was good or bad, my parents just wanted to know that it was real. This kind of parenting really helped shape me as a teenager as it allowed me to naturally climb life's learning steps without the pressure of expectation on my back at the same time. I made a lot of mistakes but it can be equally as devastating when you are living with the pressure of expectation.

It used to frustrate me when one of my classmates would receive their test back or report cards and become downcast and sad because they averaged B+ or A- when they really hoped for an A+. Now don't get me wrong, I wasn't annoyed because they had set a high standard for themselves and desperately wanted to achieve the highest grade. What upset me was the reason they wanted that A. These aspirations for high grades were hardly ever about their own goals or ambitions. It was always "My parents, my parents, my parents!" Their parents burdened them with a heavy expectation and instead of them rejoicing in the fact that they passed the test or the course. They beat themselves up because they failed their parent's expectations.

My parents expected me to do my best, but luckily they never defined my best for me. The real test in life is identifying when you've given your best effort and when you haven't. The marks on this kind of test are only shared with you internally, as this is where the desire to do better will come from. When you really think about it, it doesn't make any sense for someone else to set a standard for you because for the most part they cannot help you reach it. They can assist you, but they cannot force you. This kind of freedom really paved the way for me and even to this day, it is something I sincerely thank my parents for.

Many people might called this "liberty of learning" dangerous and they probably wouldn't be wrong. Sometimes when you don't give a sense of urgency or importance to a task, then neither will the person you're expecting to complete it. It was very easy for me to make light of all my tests and final grades knowing that my parents would not throw a fit when I got home, but it was this kind of liberated environment that personally helped me to always do my best. It's safe to say that at the end of the day, parents have just got to know the type of kids they have and how they learn best. On a side note, "Parenting 101" is not a book I'm interested in writing... yet.

My in-class experience was very special to me, and really helped shape the way I do business today. The thing is, although we may not all be academically inclined, we do all have a gift, and a unique ability to do something almost naturally. A big part of life is finding that something, and then finding a way to tie that into our life goals.

HOW?

In class, as my teachers would begin their lessons, I would try to start taking notes, answer questions and try my best to retain the information that I was learning. Seems normal right? However, in reality, I had the attention span of a 2-year old. I quickly found myself zoning out and preparing my first 'ice breaker' joke to disrupt the class during the quiet times. Actually, all the time.

The awesome part is that 99% of the time, it worked! I was actually able to target the right times, formulate the right words and affect the right people to cause a chain reaction in the class. Sometimes, I even managed to throw my teachers off guard, and even they could not deny, that what I did or said was really funny, and they would start laughing themselves. Sure I got kicked out of class quite a bit, but the fact that I would naturally keep doing this and that it kept working began to teach me something about me and about the people around me. What I realized about myself is that I naturally studied people. I was like an anthropologist or psychologist and I didn't even know it. It was effortless for me. I was able to tell when people were focused and didn't want to be interrupted, but at the same time, I could also tell when perhaps everyone needed a comical relief or a break in focus to feel at ease and recapture the bliss of who they are and where they are. This golden skill would very soon become one of the most profitable skills in my business regarding customer service. In my business today, everyday is high school and I'm the 'class clown' all over again. This doesn't necessarily mean that I just crack jokes all day with customers. Ok, maybe it does.

I try my best to read the obvious signs that customers naturally provide me, to make the best and most-tailored experience for them. This includes their body language, vocal tone, and even the colour of their clothing. Did they come alone or did they come with others? Working to understand these different aspects of a person and how they communicate can actually help to determine how each customer's experience is going to play out in a very unique way that is special to them.

We especially apply this skill to potential new customers. Remember a first impression is always a lasting one, so this is where we have majored and have noticed great success in our venture. Every new customer that comes into our store, whether they purchase a product or not, is welcomed with a grand curtsy and twirl, treated with a Swiss chocolate, and showered with attention and love. It has become the *"T By Daniel Way."*

So, how do we determine if we are about to make a first impression? It's actually quite simple. From the moment someone walks in, if they are not used to our loud welcoming greetings, or if they just aimlessly stare at the menu and ask us for a plain green tea, we know that this is a new person, who has never been to our store or tried our products. It's safe to say that 99% of the time we're right and once we welcome them in song and dance, that person is impressed and most importantly, comes back.

Our regular customers have adapted to the *"T By Daniel Way."* They're familiar with our style of greeting and the experience of just opening the door and standing at the counter while we take them on an adventurous ride through tea and all the magical things that our store has to offer.

As a class clown, I have always paid attention to these small details in people. It made me wonder, was the A+ student smarter than I was because they were paying attention to the "important" information that they would need to ace the test? Was I destined for failure, because I would naturally hear and focus on this so-called "un-important" information?

In my opinion, there is a benefit to both types of people. In class, the teacher would say things like, "If we understand the lesson being taught and apply it, then we would pass our courses and eventually be the most likely person that an employer would hire for the required

HOW?

position." The A+ student would then get excited about this potential educational advancement, take notes and study it until they mastered it. Sure enough, they succeeded. As the teacher promised, they graduated school with honours and they did get the job.

On the other hand there was me, who thought, "What if I am the employer? Do I still need to take notes right now? Would I seriously even care about these "skills" if I were the one hiring someone?" I explored these thoughts and studied this way of thinking. The result? I too got excited, but not about landing a job. My excitement came from the thought of potentially being the owner. Sure enough, through time, maturity and experience I mastered it. As the teacher expected, I didn't graduate school with honours and I didn't get the dream job. instead, I created it.

Ok, we've laughed. We've chuckled. We've broken some rules. We've learned a little something from a class clown. But what if you're a lawyer, an accountant, or a divorce consultant? These are obviously more serious industries, which present very few opportunities for humour. So how does this 'class clown' theory still apply to you?

Well, being a class clown doesn't necessarily mean making jokes. It's actually more about getting to know people, and looking at the signs that they're providing you. It's about hearing what they're not saying and customizing their experience to suit their personality, instead of always following the protocol. You'll find that you become far more memorable than the other companies that they visit on any given day, that think great customer service is collecting their money and saying have a nice day, please come again. Be less robotic, and instead focus on being more human.

So what's the final take home here? Simple.
The path often taken is not the only path. It's just the most popular one. And although it can feel safer to take the

main road, you will forever be haunted by the thought of the road less travelled. The one that puts you out of your comfort zone, and the one that questions everything you know and have been taught. That road that could lead to both everything and nothing. That's how I felt walking away from St Augustine that day. I didn't know what my next move was going to be, but boy was I glad to take off that uniform and hang it up forever.

 Sincerely,

The high school dropout.

MAN OF STEEL...TOED BOOTS.

Wouldn't it be cool to be a super powerful, flying alien that looks human, like Superman? There have been many times in life where I felt like flying away to another planet, and my desires for a red cape and an alter ego were getting stronger. At this point, the natural repercussions of dropping out of school began to set in. I was education-less, jobless; I had a criminal record and only the mere hopes of becoming a signed recording rap artist. My future looked bleak.

My supportive, successful and balanced parents, started to give me that "what are you doing with your life" look as they would see me at home everyday trying to figure life out. More than anything I think they were concerned with the path I had chosen, but despite how bad it looked, there was a confidence behind their concern. They lived by example and their strong morals mixed with their faith in Jesus Christ, would always assure them that eventually everything would fall into place and things would work out for their children.

Day after day I would spend hours in my home-based recording studio trying to sing, rap and write my way into success, but as more time would pass the responsibilities of life were becoming more and more real to me.

I needed an income and therefore I needed a job, and I needed it fast! How else would I continue to fund my music dreams? Where would I get the money to print my own CD covers? How would I afford to continue putting gas in my car, or go out with my friends? These are the little realities that started to drown out my music dreams. I started to realize that I wasn't a child anymore and I could no longer pretend that my parents were always going to bail me out and everything was always going to work out for me whether I took control of my life or not.

Thus, the job hunt began. I began printing a ton of resumes and tried my best to customize them to whichever job I was applying to, but nobody would call back. I tried malls, fast food restaurants and office cleaning, I was willing to pretty much take anything and go anywhere. But luck did not seem to be on my side. I was confused. I felt like a colourblind boy holding a Rubik's Cube for the first time. I couldn't quite figure out how to piece life together.

After two months of searching I became aware of a few local job agencies that apparently hire people like myself who are looking for extra cash and temporary work. It was so simple. There were no special requirements, no academic must haves and no real work experience necessary. All I had to do was sign up; tell them when I'd like to work, take a short WHMIS training test and *ba da boom*! I finally got a new job. And this wasn't just any job. It was perfect in every way. I could work and earn money for my music dream and I could leave the job at any point if the music started to take off. I was easily replaceable at the agency and I loved that.

Ever heard the saying when something sounds too good to be true, it probably is? Well let's put it this way. My first day on the job was my last day.

The moment I walked into my new job I hated it. I hated the way I felt. I hated the environment of the warehouse and I hated the fact that I had to stay there for eight hours.

HOW?

I hated the smell, the tasks and most of all; I hated those big steel-toed boots! The general labour-warehouse atmosphere was everything that I wasn't. As I walked into the factory and located my shift supervisor, I was immediately told where to put my lunch bag and where to clock in for my shift. After those meticulous instructions, I was guided into the warehouse where I was introduced to my trainer.

"Hey buddy, you the new guy?"

"Yes," I replied.

"Good, grab a bin and start picking the items on this list."

In my head I started thinking, maybe I've landed on some strange, undiscovered planet where people don't have names and salutations are evil. Superman, are you here? Anyways, I was never one to make a big deal out of uncomfortable situations, so I just sucked it up and started hunting for all the listed items. My goal? Make the unhappy, no-name trainer happy. Right, like that was possible.

After eight grueling hours had finally gone by, I was surprisingly very exhausted. I would have never thought that such a simple job could be so tiring, but it was. That night I got home and used the scary reality of having to go back to that warehouse for the rest of my life as motivation to write and record two or three songs. My hope was that at the very least, I might just stumble upon some magical one hit wonder. Negative.

I called the agency and let them know that I wouldn't be returning to that job for some made up reason and that they should call me if something else came up. Time went on and the agency would call every now and then and I would take some jobs, try some jobs, and quit some jobs. This was my new life: Daniel, the job hopper.

Although I initially hated factory work, over time I started to take a more positive approach to general labour by changing my perspective about what the word actually means. General labour is usually work that requires physical strength and stamina rather than skill or training. Don't get me wrong, there are many general labour positions that actually require intensive training, but the positions I was landing were just the good old "using the hands" kind of work.

Sounds fairly simple, but these jobs were no walk in the park. There were some people who had been working those positions for 15-20 years without ever missing a shift. They spent hours on their feet, keeping up with super sonic productions lines and paying attention to the tiniest of details. Talk about an undercover superhero. This was hard work and hard work could not be taught. You can't just schedule someone in for a three hour "hard work" training shift. This quality of work had to be in your blood. You had to want it, and you had to see every drop of sweat as a reward and every lunch break as a necessity rather than a desire. Now if at this point you forgot, I am still talking about a general labour job. If you feel like you just tuned into the newest motivational Nike commercial, you kind of just did. This is the way I started to view general labour and hard work on a whole. I had to work like I was born to do it, almost like it was my calling. This is when life got interesting. My whole perception on working was changed and the fire to work very hard had been ignited. My co-workers did their job like it was easy and enjoyable. You would never catch them standing around complaining and watching the clock counting down the minutes until the next break. They did what they had to do with no excuses.

The next few months could easily become another book all by itself. That book would be called something like "Welcome To The Grind." I signed up for every agency known to man, or at least known to my city. I wanted to work so badly, with no real goal in mind other than to change my situation I guess. Agencies were calling and sending me everywhere. I was working two and sometimes even three job placements at a time, some

HOW?

overnights, some early mornings and sometimes I would finish one job and head right to the next. I became so well known at all the agencies, that I started to get permanent job offers rather than temporary placements. This was good, and the money was great. I even bought another car and I began to feel like I had a life again. I thought to myself, it's time to take this new work ethic and apply it to my aspiring music career. Oh, you thought I had given up on that? Not a chance. I was going to outwork every other aspiring artist. I started staying up late searching the web for key people in the industry and trying to find their emails or a contact number. I even wrote down all the addresses of the major record labels and paid them an unexpected visit. I emailed A&R's and invited them out to local shows where I would be performing. I started to create my story and intensify my hustle, thinking back to my general labour inspiration and the ball started rolling.

I began doing a lot of research about tips on what made a successful music artist. I stumbled upon some information about a music manager. I soon came to understand that behind every great artist was an even greater manager. The manager was usually someone who understood the artist's vision, style and direction and steered them into the right connections. This person also took care of all the business aspects of a music career, like bookings, inquiries, interviews, sales, accounting, and all the other boring stuff. I just wanted to rap; I didn't want to worry about things like answering phones. But how on earth could I afford a real manager? I was just making enough to live, and I certainly wasn't at any place to hire anyone. Then, it hit me. My manager was going to have to be someone who just believed in me. Someone who knew that I would work hard, and that I was willing to never give up and do whatever it takes to make it big. If my manager could stick with me during the beginning stages, when I struck it big, it would pay off for them big time.

I continued working and writing music while working my

agency jobs, and my hard work, and music did end up catching someone's attention: My loyal friend Chad. Chad loved my music! He would take my cd's and play them in his car, and share them with other people. Pretty soon, every time I wrote and recorded a new song, I would burn it on a cd, call Chad, and we would sit in his car, turn up the speakers and just take it in. Chad was more than enthusiastic about all of my punch lines and my style of rapping. He was my first, and probably my only real fan.
So naturally, he joined the hustle. Chad became my official personal artist manager. As you know, Chad was everything but shy, and was not afraid to talk to people and knock on doors. He started soliciting my music and artist press kits to everyone. He believed I was the next big artist to blow up and he wasn't going to miss a beat, literally.

I began devoting a lot of time to my music. I would stay up all night writing songs and trying to find beats. Little by little, my music dreams started to become reality as I started carving out a name for myself in the industry. Meanwhile, on the other hemisphere of my life I started calling in "sick" quite often and once again my job placements began to wither away.
Insert lesson on work-life balance here.
A beautiful quote from Alain de Botton says, "There is no such thing as work-life balance. Everything worth fighting for unbalances your life." This couldn't be truer.

Now with my music dreams on the rise and my new work ethic in full gear, becoming a signed recording artist for once didn't seem impossible. In fact it was closer than ever. We were constantly sending out emails, MySpace inbox messages, and thinking of creative ways we could get our name out there. We struck GOLD one fine day when we a got an inbox message from a representative for a U.K based rap duo called S.A.S expressing their interest in a collaboration. To offer some perspective, this is the equivalent of winning the lottery in the rap world. A known artist, wanted to collaborate with us? Was I dreaming?

S.A.S stood for "Streets All Salute" or "Straight Across Seas" as they were said to be respected no matter which country, neighbourhood or street they found themselves in. S.A.S also known as the Dipset Euro Gang were the British affiliates of the umbrella hip hop label in Harlem, New York known as Dipset. All in all, the entire Dipset regime was a side label owned by internationally acclaimed rap superstar Jay-Z, founder and lead artist of Roc-A-Fella Records. Of course, in our anxious little minds we felt that by making a record with S.A.S we were in some way associated with Jay-Z, even if in the smallest way.

The collaboration contract included a featured song and a live performance with us, at a local nightclub outside of Toronto. This means we would write a song, they would feature on it and then we'd go perform it together. We were on top of the world! We believed that this was our break. This was our moment and we weren't going to let anything or anyone get in our way. Except money. Unfortunately it managed to get in our way. The price tag on this collaboration with S.A.S including flights, hotel accommodations and the rider list (which is a list of requests and demands from the artist to enhance their comfort while travelling) came to a whopping twelve thousand dollars and we had a very short period of time to send it. Excuse me while I faint.

Although this doesn't sound like an out of this world amount of money, when you're nineteen with no savings, and never having seen more than a seven hundred dollar pay cheque every two weeks, the thought of coming up with this money in a week, felt just next to impossible. But when you're ambitious, self- driven, confident or just straight up crazy, you're going to find a way to make it work, and we did. If I never knew how to go about borrowing money, I was about to learn it the hard way.

First, we decided to sell the few possessions that we had

which were mainly our cars. Second, we all contributed any savings that we had put away in any bank accounts and also added our current pay cheques if anyone was working at the time. Third, we went to our families and tried to express the importance of the opportunity at hand while giving them hope of the positive, successful future that would result from this. When the dust had settled and we had scraped everything we could together, we were still short three thousand dollars. So now what? Friends, acquaintances and even strangers who kind of had an idea of what we were doing then became our last option and in a very dreadful way, life was going to teach me what a venture capitalist or investor actually was.

One of my friend's cousins heard that we were on the come up rappers and we had a potential gig opportunity to record a song and perform with S.A.S. Because of Dipset's popularity in the rap industry at the time, he could foresee that this could be something big. I'll call this distant acquaintance Charlie, simply because to this day, I'm not totally sure what his name actually is. My rap group and I met with Charlie a few times and explained to him exactly what we were planning to do and also the potential turnout that we could expect at the nightclub if we went ahead with the collaboration. I could immediately sense that Charlie was able to help us out because of his evident interest and the flashy cars and clothes that he would always be seen in. Let's put it this way- Charlie had money to spare and it was obvious. Our convincing worked and a few days after meeting with Charlie, he simply called up my friend, met with him and gave him the total outstanding money that we needed to go ahead with the collaboration. He also mentioned to him that we would owe him a small interest on top of the borrowed money once the event was over. WHAT! Just like that?

This was amazing and my dream of becoming a famous rap artist just got a lot closer. I felt like we had just found our first real investor or someone that must really believe in what we were doing. After we paid S.A.S's management and got the ball rolling, I felt really good. But I couldn't help but wonder in the back of my mind, how was Charlie able to get and giveaway that much money so fast? I mean initially I thought he must have an amazing job, maybe at one of those top-notch factories that pay big money, but then that didn't make sense because he was always out driving his fancy cars. Maybe he had rich parents…. well not quite because he didn't live with his parents either. And then, like a brick to the head, it all became clear to me. Charlie was a different kind of hustler. A candy man, a street pharmacist…if you catch my drift. Boy oh boy, did I just do a deal with the devil.

We spent the next few weeks trying our best to write an original song, sending it back and forth to our new British friends. After a few attempts the song was recorded, and S.A.S came to Canada. We booked them into a luxury suite at the One King West Hotel in Toronto, and our big performance was scheduled at a nightclub just outside of Toronto in a city called Burlington. From this experience I really got to see first hand how most people only care about money and once that was taken care of, nothing else really matters. Don't get me wrong, S.A.S were pretty cool guys, but in all reality, they were someone and we were no one. So the excitement that we felt riding in a limo with them and hanging out with them in Downtown Toronto for a few days, was not necessarily mutual. Nevertheless, we lived the life of a rock star for a few days and it was amazing. The big night of the performance arrived and if there was ever a time I had butterflies in my stomach it was then. I couldn't believe what was about to happen. I was about to share the stage with an international signed rap duo, and about to perform an original song. My friends and I suited up in the best Bathing Ape hoodies we could find, got fresh haircuts and recited our lyrics over and over to make sure that we didn't mess up any of our lines.

I guess no matter how sweet a dream is; eventually you have to wake up. But in my case this dream was about to turn into a nightmare that could not be easily shaken by just waking up. As we entered the smoky stage and looked out, my heart sank. My longing eyes stared out into a huge empty nightclub, and the stinging feeling of failure began to eat away at my insides. This was not the sold out event I had hoped for, and I could practically name every single person in the audience, which was comprised of mainly friends, supporters and acquaintances with very few actual S.A.S fans in attendance. Our promotional skills must have seriously sucked. To make matters even worse, when it came time for S.A.S to come up on stage with us to perform the song we made with them, they no showed. Perhaps they were demotivated by the poor turnout or maybe they were off having fun with the groupies. Whatever the case was, we performed the song solo. First real investment #failed. What had become a dreaded night had finally come to a close and some of my friends had been in charge of getting S.A.S back to their hotel room. Oh yeah, we did end up finding them. I was also in charge of something, something quite serious. I had been assigned the gracious duty of counting the money and explaining to Charlie that we were nowhere close to making back any of the money that he lent us. Try telling a drug dealer that you don't have his money and let me know how that works out for you. When I had to face him, he was fuming and demanded that we give him everything that we made that night. The problem was, we were still responsible for paying the other 50% installment to the club venue that was also looking for their money. When choosing your battles in life we thought it was probably best to choose the club owner instead of the drug dealer, so we did.

The following days were brutal and super depressing. Our one big shot completely failed, our group spirit was at an all-time low, and Charlie still wanted his money. We had already exhausted all of our borrowing options so there

HOW?

was no plan B on standby. Since I was the leader of the rap group, all the weight fell heavily on me. For some reason in Charlie's eyes, it was as if I personally owed him money. He looked at the situation as if I was the only person responsible for the debt because I should have been better or been famous by now. It was terrible. The only thing I could do was ask Charlie to give us some more time to pay, as I scrape together a few pay cheques and hopefully come up with the money. Three weeks had gone by and Charlie was still not paid. I was a little more at ease because I figured he had settled down and realized that we were definitely going to pay him but it would take a little time. Well, not quite.

One night as I was working on the cook line at a restaurant with my friend, one of the other line cooks who had just come in from having a smoke called out to me and said, "Daniel, there's somebody at the back that wants to see you." This was normal for me as all of my friends used to come to the back door and chat with me for a few minutes during my shift, so I headed outside. My friend accompanied me as he too thought it was one of our mutual friends just coming to waste some time for a bit. But to my great surprise as soon as we got outside, Charlie was standing there and in the most aggressive tone with words I wouldn't even want to write, he shouted:
"Where is my money!?" I quickly answered, "We asked you to give us a little time." Before I could finish another word, Charlie pulled out what looked like a massive black cell phone and before I knew it, I was starring down the barrel of a gun. Completely startled, I quickly backed up to the restaurant wall as my friend began to panic shouting "What are you doing? Put that away, just give us some time!"

Charlie didn't want to hear what my friend had to say and I just remained quiet as the gun was pointed directly in my face. My thinking was paralyzed, I couldn't make sense out of anything, and so I just kept staring at the gun. After

Charlie went on ranting and backing me up into the wall while he threatened me, he finally concluded by saying "I better have my money in the next two days," and he took the handgun and whipped me across my face splattering blood all over my chef jacket and then he ran off. My friend quickly ran over to me panicking and asking if I was ok, as I stood there holding my bleeding nose and crying. The cry wasn't so much the physical pain that I was feeling. It was more the pressure of the entire situation and how it naturally fell on me. After I regained my composure, I told my friend to go back inside and make it known that I was having a nosebleed so that I could explain the bloody chef coat and my absence from the line for so long. He went inside and prepared the way for me to come in and I came in holding my nose and headed straight for the washroom. I don't clearly remember what we did or how we did it, but Charlie received his money in two days and that situation was put to rest. This was the Dragon's Den deal from hell and it turned me off from borrowing money at a very early stage in my life. This incident would become one of the main reasons I started my company T By Daniel from the grassroots with no bank loans or credit cards. We bootstrapped the business with mine and my wife's personal money and part-time jobs. With music behind me once again, I was refocused on simply finding a good job or two and just working to make a living. I had ruined my good rapport with most of the agencies as I kept quitting or no showing in order to attend important music functions or opportunities. However, I just had to get myself back on my feet. Let the résumé rampage begin!

JOBS, JOBS, JOBS!

Part One: The Restaurant Stint

My dad taught me to view a nine to five job as my own business. He said when you think about it, you wake up and go to work, you earn a paycheque every two weeks and when the money comes in, you are responsible for accounting for every dollar. Now I know there are a million differences between actually running your own business in comparison to working a job, but I saw the value in what he was saying. Having the discipline, ambition and leadership skills of a business owner with a nine to five job could really be a good way to structure my finances, and would give me a much healthier outlook on my day to day life. If nine to five jobs were actually businesses, then I had already owned quite a few.

Aside from my general labour experiences, I actually became quite skilled in the food and restaurant industry from the McDonald's days until now. I had held down a few restaurant jobs and I learned a lot about the food business without even realizing it. Food had always been one of my secret passions. I mean I had never really focused on it the way I focused on music or fashion in the past, but it was something I genuinely enjoyed every time I found myself working around it. I loved tasting food, smelling food, cooking food and just everything about it. With this genuine, untapped appreciation for food, I figured I'd pick myself back up again and find a job in some sort of food establishment. It was better than general labour as restaurants are typically more fast paced, making your shifts go by faster. I had applied for a job at a restaurant called Casey's. When I was applying, the only available position of course, was probably the worst position you could hold at a restaurant- a dishwasher. No, not exactly the type of food affiliation I was hoping for, but I wasn't about to complain. I took my dad's advice for once and went right into that dish pit at Casey's and transformed it into my little paradise. I would sing songs all night while power washing the disgusting left overs of chicken parmesan and fettuccini alfredo. I was infamous for flirting with all the pretty servers when they came to drop off their empty plates. Go figure. Every now and then, I would also peek my head around the cooking line and beg the chef and line cooks to make me an extra steak, or ask the dessert makers to whip me up a warm apple crumble. Eventually, my positive view about work mixed with an outgoing personality and constantly nagging the chef landed me a position on the line as a salad maker and dessert chef and out of the dish pit. If you've ever read the story in the Bible, I was beginning to feel like Joseph and the colourful coat as he worked his way up in Egypt. Having the opportunity to actually work on the line gave me a first hand look at what it actually took to be a great line cook and run a restaurant. Communication was key, and everyone no matter how great or small played a vital role. The main cook was responsible for calling out all the orders that servers were punching in for their guests via a small chit machine that seemed like it never stopped printing. The chef had to be loud, quick and organized at the same time. They had to listen carefully to the special requests coming from the servers while at the same time getting estimated preparation times on the different foods that the line cooks were making. The chef had to make sure the line cooks were acknowledging the food items when they would call them out or else this could result in a guest not getting their food in a timely fashion, or in the worst-case scenario, not get their food at all.

    I continued to work hard and focus and I began to move my way up the line again. I went from salads and desserts to appetizers and from there I went on to the

HOW?

sauté station, then on to the grill and from the grill, I actually became the main line cook on certain nights. I worked hard, I exercised leadership skills and I would even rap and sing while working on many occasions. My fellow employees seemed to enjoy working with me and I was having a blast. After many months at Casey's I moved onto another Casey's location as new management came in and changed the Casey's I came to know and love. For the next few years, I worked at various different restaurants. Everything from Chinese food to fancy wine and dine spots.

Part Two: The Fancy Salesman

I also managed to get some experience in sales when I landed a part time position with The Toronto Star Newspaper. I had a little experience from my youth with newspaper routes but sales and delivery are two different ball games. Tay, my friend who helped me start the clothing line in high school, was looking for work at the same time and I referred him to the position and he was also hired. Is it a little strange to you that every job I ever worked at, I always ended up working with my friends? It's a little weird to me too now that I'm writing about it. Anyways, every Saturday morning, my supervisor would pick Tay and I up along with a few other people in his minivan. I think he may have been Sri Lankan, or maybe from India, but as we would drive off to our route he would blast on repeat one of the most high-pitched Indian songs I had ever heard. I couldn't understand one word the singer was saying but after months of this routine, I started to actually like the song and strangely I felt like I was beginning to understand it. He would take us all over the city, drop us in a random neighborhood and we were expected to start knocking doors and trying to get subscribers to sign up for the Toronto Star Newspaper. There were some people who were kind enough to give me the time of day to give them my spiel, but for the most part, who really wants to listen to a newspaper spiel in the middle of the day. During my newspaper sales days, I experienced many doors slammed in my face. I remember thinking how amazing it is that the Toronto Star was such a big and successful publication in Canada but at the bottom of the chain, there are people like me getting doors shut in my face, regardless of my affiliation with them.

This was a humbling lesson for me as it taught me that consumers are not always impressed by a brand or a name when it comes to the products and services they want. It doesn't matter how successful the company may be or how much money they spent on their latest marketing campaign. If they didn't want your product or your service, you may get a slammed door to the face. In sales, however, you can't take it personal. There are many factors that potential customers take into consideration when it comes to making a purchase. Having this understanding in business is what separates a good sales person from a terrible one. So was I a good sales person? Judging by my low closing rate of subscriptions at the Toronto Star, I don't think I could comfortably say that I was a talented sales rep. Bye-bye Toronto Star, time for me to blast off!

If you want to learn how to grow a tree the right way, go to a forest. If you want to learn how to be a good salesman, go to a car dealership. Believe me, you'll see the great, the terrible and the in-between. Next up, I cruised my way into the car industry landing a job at a Honda dealership. However, I wasn't a car salesman. I wasn't a mechanic. And no, I wasn't even the receptionist. Ladies and gentlemen, I was the lot jockey. What is a lot jockey? Well, my job was to wipe the cars in the showroom and outside in the lot and to do occasional trades with other dealerships. I was like the little fly on the wall. I saw everything, heard everything, and due to my job description I touched everything too, just a little pointless fact I thought I'd throw in. The car dealership I was hired

HOW?

at was part of a huge auto mall, where almost every single brand of cars had a dealership on the same street. The Honda happened to be right next to a Lexus dealership, who had recently hired a new car jockey for their lot as well. Want to take a random guess at who this new car jockey was? I know it may sound like I'm making up crazy coincidences, but they hired Chadwin. And so we worked next to each other once again like back in the McDonald's days. After a few weeks of shining and moving cars, Chad and I decided to create a little hideout where we would meet on our lunch breaks to talk about life, our dreams, our employers and how much we both hoped that someday things would change for us and we could finally put an end to the job-hopping madness. We called this little hideout, "SECRET SOCIETY!" It was located behind the big green garbage dumpster at the back of the Honda car lot, where nobody ever ventured out. Chad and I came up with a secret hand gesture that we would do to notify the other person that it was time to head over to secret society. We would make two solid fists with our hands parallel to each other (as if you were giving someone a bear hug) leaving an 'S' – like shape in the middle. That meant, shine your last car, give a good sweep and be at "SS" in about five minutes. Such losers. Of all the things you can learn about in a car dealership, one key fundamental skill was sales. A car dealership showroom is like a fish tank, with hungry fish waiting for any sign of food dropping into the water. At a first glance, you would think that the fish that hang around closest to the surface of the water would be the most successful to get the food when it drops, but at the Honda dealership, this was far from the truth. The most successful salesman never confronted customers as soon as they came into the dealership. They would simply greet them with a warm, welcoming smile and walk right by them. They would then begin to engage in conversation with another team member or mechanic close by. I remember thinking to myself, this was terrible customer service. Why wouldn't they immediately assist the customers and answer their questions and show them cars. Then again what did I know; I was the failed newspaper sales boy at this point. I figured I would mind my own business and keep shining the showroom cars. After a few minutes had gone by and the customers would become comfortable enough to open a few car doors and pop a few trunks, the salesman would then approach the customer and break the ice with a confident joke or witty comment like "If you really like this one, I'll buy it for you!" or "Hey man, you're not old enough to drive this." These small icebreakers made the customers laugh almost every time and immediately slip into a comfortable conversation with the salesman. The salesman would then ask two or three questions about the most important features the car had to have and then ease back and allow the customer to tell their whole life story. As I wiped, I listened. After about fifteen minutes, the conversations no longer sounded like anyone was planning to buy or sell a car at all. It was about college and university, or about music, or the customer and the salesman going back and forth about why this team has a better chance of winning the Stanley Cup over this team or why this American president was a better leader. But surprisingly, no chatter about cars. This didn't make any sense to me, so eventually I relocated to another car somewhere else to hunt for more fingerprints so I didn't look like I was just wiping the same car for thirty minutes. Time would pass and I would always find some reason to go outside and do something just so I wasn't constantly in my manager's sight. An hour would go by and I would see the person or couple or family that was talking to the salesman eventually say their goodbyes and leave the showroom. I didn't see them sit down at the sales desk or go for any test drives, so I knew they didn't buy a car. A week later, I would come in for my shift and lo and behold, who do you think is sitting at the salesman's desk signing papers and celebrating their new car? You got it, the same customer who was chatting for an hour about nothing car related. Internally, I retracted everything I said and thought about the salesman. I realized that a good salesman is not about being a hungry fish. Being a good salesman was actually more of a social skill than a technical one. TV always made salesmen look like a sharp shooter, 3 piece suit wearing, smooth talking character that only mastered the skill after being in sales for years, but in reality it simply wasn't true. The best car salesman and the most successful ones at Honda were the ones that were good listeners, good conversationalists and likeable people who just so happen to be assisting you in purchasing a vehicle. Yes, they have to know about the cars and be able to answer your questions, but this didn't mean they had to be robotic or super formal with their approach. You could still be genuine and be yourself while making a big sale.

In my experience running my own business, I can't count how many times I received a comment from our customers proclaiming that I am a skilled salesman. I really appreciate it when I hear it, but to be quite honest, it baffles me sometimes. What people consider a good salesman is simply me just being humorous or witty or charming, or poking fun. I have learned that once people feel entertained, whether that means that they are acknowledged, listened to or even literally entertained by your service and personality, then they feel more comfortable to spend money on something they want, like or need. My business has been experiencing a steady, healthy 33% growth in sales for the last four years. How did the bad newspaper salesman manage to do this?

The great thing about starting a business is you can really cater the experience to your own personality instead of molding into someone else's ideals. I am still the class clown, the fashion designer and the aspiring musician. I wrap up everything that is truly me and sell tea in the most genuine way I can. Business is more like theatre to me and the main product is me. My guests come to see the movie because supposedly the reviews so far have been great. Another bonus about this movie is that it's free and nothing beats free. If you're still following my analogy, then you'll understand that my job is to entertain my customers. I do this by creating magical experiences for them every time they walk through our doors. The entertainment that I give to my beloved customers is free. I don't charge extra to dance around in a Buzz Light-year costume- true story. I certainly don't charge a fee to run around my city in a red cape and blue leotards proclaiming to be "SuperDan" (a tanned Superman knock off who offers tea samples to whoever I manage to fly into…or rather, run into), I do this because I love to do it, and I do it because it's real to me.

Just like in a real theatre, as patrons are enjoying the movie, it is very normal that someone will get up and visit the concession stands to purchase popcorn, a soda, cotton candy or a chocolate bar, something to go alongside with the movie experience. This something extra is our tea. We don't make sales because we offer products to our customers. We make sales because we offer a great experience, which our customers decide to pair with our products. This is the value added and this is what makes a great movie, I mean a great salesman.

THE LAST NAIL

As with all my jobs, my lot jockey days were numbered. I had a bad run in with my manager, who ended up sharing a few words with me that were not exactly friendly. I figured I didn't need to put up with anyone's disrespect and I quit Honda. However at this point I was 20 years old and I really needed to keep myself employed. I decided to sign up to an agency to get something quickly. However, what I did end up getting was the last general labour position that I would ever set foot into. Ever!

When the first day at my newest general labour gig arrived, I have to admit I was actually pretty excited about this new opportunity and ready to get my hands back to the grind. The pay was very attractive, it was summertime, and my brother along with another friend also got hired. It was the perfect way to get myself back on my two feet.

As we arrived to the warehouse, we did the usual routine sign up and tour of the facility, but something was off. There was no trainer and nobody who looked like they were delegated to walk with us and show us around to let us know exactly what we were in charge of. Just a man, who looked like maybe the owner, or the manager, leading us through the warehouse. I thought, how come we didn't get any briefing or a quick "how to" on the job we would be doing? Weird, but whatever. Maybe the job wasn't that difficult.

We continued to walk through the factory, which didn't look much different then you're average warehouse setting. As the manager guy continued to lead us around, my brother and I looked at each other and gave a brief sigh of relief, happy that we were in this together.
"Alright guys, here's your new job."
And there it was. Tall, huge, and silver in colour. The bin.
The big, rustic steel bin that you can usually see attached to the back of a truck transporting stones, salt or some other minuscule natural resource. I thought to myself, this is strange, why was our supervisor leading us inside of a bin? Was this a trap? Was this a secret passage to some underground warehouse where we would really be working? I was honestly waiting for Ashton Kutcher to jump out and scream Punk'd! and a hidden camera crew to jump out from behind some corner. But this was no TV show. This was very real. I would be spending the next eight hours of my life in a big steel bin. Ever heard the saying "When it rains it pours?" Well it's true. I soon came to realize that working in the bin was not what made this situation really bad. It was the items inside of the bin that was the real torture. I felt like I was walking into a jail cell all over again as I entered into the steel prison, which was literally filled with tiny nails, screws and bolts. There were trillions of them; I mean quadrillions of these little mini metal monsters.

"I'll be needing you young men to sort these screws and bolts." Said the supervisor.
 Sorry, let me just grab a handkerchief to dry the tears off my face before I write the next sentence. My new job was to sort all the tiny screws and nails into little containers, until the big, tall bin was empty. Yes, empty. Imagine someone sent you to Mars and told you to gather planet dust and filter it into little containers starting from the tiniest pebble to the biggest rock. That's what this felt like.

HOW?

I used Mars as an example because I believe this job should only be offered to people who are crazy enough to live on Mars. Seriously? Sorting screws and nails?

I looked at my brother, and my friend, and then looked back at the steel bin, and for a moment we just stood in silence. After we regained our composure, we got straight to work. All you could hear ascending out of the big steel bin was *klink-klink*, which was the sound of metal fragments hitting other metal fragments as we were scooping up screws and nails. This sound was mixed with occasional bursts of laughter, as my friend, my brother and I somehow found some comedic relief in the situation, as we looked at the amount of work that was before us.

"Don't stress guys!" I would tease.

"We only have about eighty-thousand more nails left."

As we laughed and joked, I thought for a moment, it's not really that bad. We were basically just sorting things, plus we are getting paid very well, and we're all together. So what's the big deal? We could do this! I'm glad you admired my optimism because so did I. But it did not last very long. At about the sixth hour of our shift, fatigue hit me in a very discouraging way. Our pace had slowed down, the laughing came to a halt and with so much time to think, I was again faced with the reality of all my poor decisions in life. To make matters just a little worse, the warehouse lot we worked at wasn't too far from the Toronto Pearson Airport, so all day we were taunted by colourful little airplanes, full of fortunate people flying to beautiful places all over the world. As the planes passed, I remember seeing one particular airplane fly right over us. It seemed to have caught all of our attention, as we all stopped, stood, and looked up.

My friend spoke our mind as he mumbled, "Man, that should be us." Jon and I didn't even respond to his comment and just got back to sorting nails, but it wasn't because we didn't agree with what he said, it was just that, well, we really messed up. Private jets, business travel, nice cars, classy restaurants and all that glamorous stuff was for the people in life that worked hard. It was for people who were consistent. People who went to school. People who didn't mess up on big opportunities. It wasn't for people like me who dropped out of high school to start rapping in my basement. It wasn't for a guy like me who had no diploma or valuable skills to offer. It wasn't for the guy who had the opportunity of a lifetime to make a record with a signed artist and somehow managed to do nothing with it. At that moment, I think we were all silently sharing the same thoughts. *"Klink- Klink- Klink."* That was the sound of steel-toed boots exiting the bin. My friend decided he had had enough.

"Sorry, guys", he mumbled, "I can't do this!" And just like that he was gone. I looked at Jon and we silently agreed to just get through the shift, even though internally we too had given up. We stayed and finished the eight hours just to make sure there were no complications with our pay cheques.

Our shift was an emotional roller coaster ride. I went from laughing my head off, to sighing and dwelling on all my regrets to somehow feeling encouraged. As my thoughts gathered, I decided that I too was going to give up, but I didn't mean I was going to walk away from my job, It was a different kind of giving up. I officially gave up on failure. I determined in myself that despite all of my mistakes, I would never stand up gazing at airplanes ever again in my life wishing that I was someone that I wasn't. I would never be discouraged with how my life turned out simply because a few of life's many doors have closed on me. There was no law in life that says people with faults can never become someone great or do something great. That was a lie that I fed myself whenever I would consider my current situation, but it wasn't true. I thought to myself, what was stopping me from going home now and begin to change my situation? There was absolutely nothing.

HOW?

The only reason I wasn't seeing any different results in my life was because I wasn't doing anything different in my life. I was so stuck on making it in music, and not being qualified for anything beyond a factory or restaurant job that I blocked out every other possible opportunity to move my life forward. Yes I wanted to become a successful music artist, but was that all I could ever be in life? What's wrong with also becoming a successful business owner or an amazing author or even a pilot! There was no such thing as impossible. As the famous quote clearly states, "Even impossible says I'm-possible." All I had to do was quit boxing myself into a category of people and open up the door to possibility. Only then could the walls of all my failures come crashing down. Folks, Daniel was motivated once again! I don't know how, but I was!

They say life is not about reaching the destination, but instead it's about enjoying the journey. We all go through so many different situations in life, some good, some bad, but everything we go through is only to shape us and to prepare us for the next adventure.

I had proven to myself before that I had a very insightful skill with people from my high school days. I proved that I was a quick thinker with my freestyling abilities and creative with words from the songs I used to write. I proved to myself that I have perseverance for the things I wanted in life when I realized that I actually got a signed artist to come all the way from Great Britain to Canada. I proved to myself that I can work very hard even in undesirable situations like all my general labour experiences. I had skills. Everyone has skills, no matter what bin they might find themselves in. Why had I not paid more attention to them before? The mightiest army is not made up of a thousand strong captains. A mighty army is made up of a thousand brave soldiers who exercise their individual strengths in a mighty way. The same kind of thinking applies to us as individuals. Sometimes we break ourselves down into several weak characters, rather than pulling everything that is strong about us together to create one strong character. Mushy stuff, yes, but it's true!

I am a strong believer in God and I also believe that everything happens for a reason. Screws and nails are used to fix things, to tighten things, and to fasten things together. Perhaps God allowed me to work in this bin of nails to fix my way of thinking. Whatever the case may be, it worked. This was definitely the last nail for me.

CUT

Coincidence? In the previous chapter I talked about comparing myself to a movie and now this chapter is called cut. Totally unplanned, I promise. When I think of the making of a movie, one of the things that always stood out to me was that thing people would use on set to cut the scene and start again. I did some research while writing this book and found out that it's actually called a clapperboard or clappers. These clapperboards are typically black and white and are used to signal the beginning or the end of a movie scene. Back in the old film days, audio and video were recorded on separate machines and thus they had to find a way to accurately synchronize the audio and video to produce a perfect film. When the clapper makes that 'smack' noise it causes the audio track to dramatically spike creating an obvious start point or end point in the audio track, making it easier to align the video with it. Directors would also write the name of the movie and the scene on these clapperboards; just incase a section of the film was ever misplaced or unidentified. Pretty cool, huh? *"Smack!"*

That was me pretending to use a clapperboard to end my rambling about clapperboards and cut to the point. This part of my life was the moment where an invisible clapperboard sounded and marked the end of the first episode of my 21-year long movie.

Four years had passed since I was a rowdy high school dropout recording music in my basement and a lot had changed. I realized that the way I was going about trying to become a successful music artist probably wasn't going to work, especially because being bad was the new loser and dark shades were out of style. At this time in life, I was in between jobs so I was pretty much unemployed. I wasn't looking to just jump into any more jobs as I had talked with my parents about trying to find something that could be more stable for me. I definitely experienced some level of maturity since my seventeen-year-old days, as I was no longer causing trouble, writing rap songs until 4 a.m. or partying at the downtown nightclubs. The things I enjoyed changed drastically. I used to be someone who loved spending my Saturdays buying liquor at the LCBO and then getting wasted with all my friends. But at this point more than anything, I learned to just love food with friends and some of my best moments were created when I would grab Jon, Chad and my girlfriend Renata and head out to a local food establishment.

Around this time, my mom and dad began to serve in ministry as Pastors, which by default made me a Pastor's son. Imagine that. Growing up in Christian churches, Pastors' children always had this certain stereotype to them. In most cases, they were pretty well off, well educated, well mannered and well dressed, following the example and the path their parents had set for them. But, as you know, this was certainly not the case for my brother or myself. Our parents purposed in themselves never to force their beliefs on us. The difference between the way they lived and my own personal thoughts about Christianity was that they had somehow established a relationship with Jesus Christ rather than just a passed down religion, full of a bunch of rules and heavy demands. My parents were always the happiest and most free people I knew, but at the same time they were so dedicated to

HOW?

their faith, and so disciplined in life, work and all their other responsibilities. None of this made sense to me back then, but thankfully I have come to discover the same beautiful relationship with Jesus Christ that I saw my parents have, and He has completely changed my life today.

Nothing really changed in our home when my parents became Pastors, mainly because they were always living the kind of life you would assume Pastors would live. I think more of the change that began to happen was to my brother and myself. I remember nights where I would read my Bible and say to God, "If you just make yourself real to me, I promise I will dedicate my life to you, I just need it to be real." Many times I would read stories in the Bible and sometimes the character's life that I was reading about was so similar to mine, that I would feel encouraged when things would turn out well for them, because I thought maybe I too could experience this kind of good fortune. I sure wasn't a saint, but I was definitely warming up to the idea of living the Christian way and making this new commitment for real.

Every Wednesday evening, my parents would hold a Bible study at church and although I was reluctant to attend at first, it slowly started to become the most exciting part of my week and I loved it! We would sit down in a classroom-like setting and my dad, the Pastor, would dig out these beautiful and wise lessons from the Word of God and teach it to the congregation in the simplest way. Little by little, Christianity started making sense to me, and the more I learned the more I would realize who God really is and why it was important for me to apply what I learned to my own life.

Things were taking a very unexpected turn for me, but overall I felt this was the best change I could have made in my life and for once things seemed to be looking up. But just like in the world of business, the moment things seem to be looking up; life throws another fastball at you.

It was Wednesday, April 14, 2009 and I rolled out of bed like most 21 year olds, still sleepy after sleeping for 12 hours and very hungry. I scrambled some eggs, buttered some toast and chopped a few slices of plantain because that type of breakfast just made every morning worth waking up for. I'm not too sure what happened after breakfast but it couldn't have been that productive because I was still in my white long-sleeved sweater and grey jogging pants. Not exactly dressed for success. Chad gave me a call and said he was coming over, probably to discuss a new game plan for how we could approach the music industry, or take over the world. Chad always had the most creative, crazy and sometimes strange ideas, some of which would have been brilliant if we actually took anything other than music seriously. Since the days of Mrs. Jones English class and the hoppi-frog incident, making it in the music industry was pretty much all we ever talked about. It was becoming clear that my hip-hop dreams were not unraveling as planned. Being a person who is never really easily discouraged I thought that perhaps if it wasn't hip-hop, my dreams could still be found somewhere in music. Maybe I just needed to change my style. So when I did spend time on music I tried writing pop and pop-rock songs. Regardless of the genre, it was a refreshing adventure for us.

    I guess this would be a good time to introduce my younger sister, Rachel. My mom had her later in life and we have a fourteen-year age gap. Although we couldn't spend a lot of time together due to our huge gap in age, Jon and I really enjoyed her. She became like our baby. During high school we would rush home just to see her. In fact, I think Jon dropped out of school just to spend time with her in the day. She has always been one of the most special surprises we have ever shared in life.

Chad arrived at my house just around the same time that Rachel came home from school. She was six years old at the time. Whenever I wanted a cool random effect in any

HOW?

of my songs, I used to force her to sing or get her to record the intro for me. I thought it was a cool touch to have a child on the song because her voice was so cute and tiny and would sound really unique if I added an effect to it. Forcing Rachel into singing on my songs didn't come easily and many times bribery was required. As a reward for helping me out with some of my songs, I promised her that I would repay her in candy. It was cheaper than cutting her a cheque or offering up royalties. She would ask me for that candy every single day and I would always say I'm too busy, or too tired or simply find some reason not to go. If she were my employee, this would be the part where she would quit. But today was different.

Maybe I was inspired by something and felt the need to take a walk or maybe she just looked extra cute with her classic four-braid hairstyle and multicolored hair ties. Whatever it was, I decided that today would be the day that my Ray would be paid in full.

It was around 6:30 p.m. and Chad was still at my house. The house was a lot busier now because as I mentioned, it was a Wednesday and Wednesdays meant Bible studies. My mom and my dad were already preparing to head out as they were always extra early for church. Was it because they were the Pastors and they had to be? Or did they just master punctuality? I'm not too sure but punctuality is something that I really struggled with all my life and something I really admired in others. Rachel was also ready for church, but being that it was still a little early before they headed out she tried her luck and asked me if I was still going to get her that candy I had promised. Right before I came up with another excuse, I caught myself and instead answered, "Yes! Let's go quickly."

Chad, who was hanging out with me in the kitchen offered to come to the convenience store, which was literally, a stone's throw from my house across the street, but I told him to stay, as I wouldn't be long. At this point, after almost 10 years of friendship, Chad was like family so it wasn't a problem for me to leave him at my house while I stepped out. I pushed my feet through my sandals and took my little sister by the hand and headed for the convenience store, and that was that. A simple two-minute walk with my sister that I would never live to forget.

As we got across the street still holding hands and laughing about sweet nothings, I kept my sister excited by asking her which candy bar she was going to choose when we got to the store. We turned the corner and I saw about six guys standing in front of the convenience store leisurely hanging out around a white car with the doors opened wide. At a first glance, I didn't recognize any one that I personally knew by name, but I had definitely seen some of their faces around the neighbourhood before. As I kept looking, something about their disposition didn't feel right, and it was quite easy to observe that they were up to no good. Based on my experiences, I could just sense it. I casually walked by just about reaching for the convenient store door when one of the guys spoke out to me saying,
"Hey! Aren't you that rapper guy who said something about my friend in one of your songs?"

His tone made it clear that whatever I had said about his friend in my song could not have been something good, but I was completely caught off guard because I haven't made those kinds of songs since my high school days. The only appropriate response I could reply given I didn't really know these guys and I wasn't exactly sure what he was talking about was "Are you seriously asking me this right now? Can't you see I'm with a child?"
Offended that I would answer him in such a condescending way, he immediately eased off the white car and stepped towards me fueled by his friends chanting, "Yo! Who's this guy talking to like that?" and I knew that this was about to be a problem. All I could think about at this point was Rachel, who had no idea what was going on. She gripped my hand tightly and looked up at me with the most innocent eyes and confused and apologetic

expression on her face. That look had words and those words said, "I'm sorry for wanting the candy." Guilt was on her little face for asking me to take her to the candy store. This erupted a volcano of anger inside of me. She's a kid! She shouldn't be feeling guilty for wanting what any other six year old would want! Why does she have to be a part of this experience right now? Why are these losers still confronting me when they see me with a little child? All these thoughts raced through my head in a matter of seconds. The guy that had initially asked me the question confronted me, as I stood right at the corner of the convenience store holding Rachel's hand. The other guys that were with him stood around with a look on their face of intimidation towards me as if they were prepared to gang rush me if I decided to walk away without answering to their leader. I stood there with a straight look on my face that showed them that I wasn't scared of them, after all the times I had been in situations like this, I wasn't. The story in the Bible where David faced off against Goliath flashed through my mind. David was smaller, untrained and unarmed yet he remained confident and in the end defeated Goliath the Giant. Once again reading the Bible had proven to be helpful to me, as the memory of this story only strengthened my confidence.

"How come you're not talking now?" he taunted. "Where's your big mouth now?" He continued to provoke me insisting that I answered him as confidently as I looked.

Suddenly, I saw the front end of my parents' car pulling into the plaza where the convenience store was located and they drove up to the side of the store. They were completely oblivious to what was going on in front of them but instead came to wait for my sister to get her candy from the store so they could take her and head off to church. This was my only opportunity to get her out of harm's way. Relieved, I quickly pushed her towards my parents' parked car at the side of the building and told her,

"Go to Mommy and Daddy!" She took off crying with a panicked look on her face running towards my parent's car. With Rachel now out of the way, this immediately triggered several things. First, the guy who was confronting me now felt bold enough to step right up into my face demanding that I give him satisfaction by answering one of his taunting questions. Secondly, with Rachel now out of danger, I could properly defend myself and give it to this coward for trying to pick a fight with me while I was with my little sister. Lastly, my parents were now alerted that something was terribly wrong when they saw Rachel running towards the car crying.

He shoved me using both hands and pushed me back a step or two. I recoiled by instinct with a clenched fist to his face followed by another as he tried throwing punches back at me. We grappled and scuffled for a moment while I could see his friends standing back, watching and getting ready to escape the scene as bystanders must have been witnessing what was happening by now. As we fought I could feel how weak this guy actually was. He was just a big talker in baggy clothes empowered by the number of guys surrounding him. As we punched and wrestled I could sense that he was surprised at how much I was overpowering him. I grabbed him by his sweater to try and swing him down to the ground as I could see my parents jumping out of their car running towards me now in the middle of the parking lot. One by one, all of his friends started running away and yelling at him "Let's go! Let's go!" but he ignored them and instead took four or five more aimless punches at me. By the time he took the last punch, I had managed to pick him up and throw him down on the curb separating us and causing him to fumble around for a second or two before picking something up and running away.

My mom tried to grab a hold of him while he scrambled on the ground but she could only manage to grip his sweater as he shook her off and ran away.

HOW?

Cowards, they're always the biggest talkers and the easiest to defeat. I had clearly won the fight, but I felt strangely weak. I knew that a fight could be physically draining, but this feeling was different than any other fight I had been in before. I began stumbling and blinking repeatedly as I wobbled around the parking lot like a drunken man. My dad had been a little delayed in getting to me as he had been frantically trying to notion to my sister to remain in the car as he rushed to come and break up the fight. Why did this fight take so much out of me? He wasn't even that strong. My dad grabbed a hold of me and threw what must have been his shirt over my neck. I was confused, until I looked down at my white sweater which was now drenched in thick, red blood. I had been stabbed.

I guess in my anger and adrenaline I didn't notice the guy pull out a knife near the end of our fight and stab me four times. One was in my neck about a few millimeters from my jugular vein, one in my abdomen, one in my chest close to my underarm and one in my hand nearly slicing my pinky finger off.

It felt like hours since I had put on my sandals and headed for the convenience store, but in reality, my life had just drastically changed in the span of eight minutes. My parents grabbed onto me wrapping my body all over with garments that turned crimson red upon contact. Pardon the graphic details, but blood was dripping all over the parking lot and the sidewalk as they rushed me into the car and laid me down beside my terrified sister who was screaming and drenched in tears. I blinked and blinked and tried my best to breathe as I began feeling weaker and weaker as the seconds went by. *"Smack!"* I had been cut.

Growing up, I remember watching several talk shows such as The Montel Williams Show and The Oprah Show where guests on several occasions would try their best to explain their near death experiences. They would usually say something like, I remember seeing a bright light or a long tunnel, and I always thought that was so cliché.

Regretfully, I retracted that thought and apologize to all those guests on the show, because I too began to see that tunnel of light as I was now fighting for my own life. I realized that what seemed to be a tunnel of light was actually the natural dimming of my eyes as life was trying to escape my body. The light at the end was the final glimpse of life that I could identify as my eyes were persistent on closing for the last time. I can now certainly see how this experience would be described as a light at the end of a tunnel.

After rushing me into the car, my parents sped out of the convenience store plaza heading for the Brampton Civic Hospital when all of a sudden my dad decided to whip the car around and take me home instead. This was a very bold move, but it proved to be a much wiser decision in the end, according to the paramedics. We wouldn't have made it. Trying to drive me to hospital and having to deal with the traffic, and the constant breaking and stopping could have been fatal. It was so difficult to breathe as I could feel bubbles of air seeping out of every wound. It actually hurt to breathe so I was forced to take mini gasps of air, making me feel weaker and weaker. Twenty-one years of taking breathing for granted. I could only imagine how many other things I had taken for granted at this point. One thing was for sure, the Daniel you've gotten to know was dying, however a new Daniel was just on the verge of being born.

It was a race against time and my track and field records couldn't save me now. My parents pulled the car up on the driveway as my dad ran into the house to find some blankets that he could wrap around all the open wounds to help stop the bleeding. Unfortunately I was bleeding from four different places on my body so there was no easy solution. Instead, my dad ran outside with a large blanket and completely wrapped me inside as he and my mother began escorting me out of the blood drenched vehicle, with his hand tightly pressed against the slash on

HOW?

my neck. It was either the frantic action of my dad bursting into the house or the alarming sound of my sister crying that alerted Chad that something was wrong. He ran outside with a confused and frightened look on his face pleading that someone tell him what was going on. As Chad turned the corner of the house and stepped onto the driveway, he immediately saw me covered in blood and blankets and overwhelmed and confused, Chad fainted on the driveway.

Years later and even during the writing of this book, as Chad retells me what he saw and how he felt at that very moment, it sends chills throughout my body. Chad told me that up until that day he had never fainted before or experienced what it was like to black out. He explained that a feeling erupted in his toes and in seconds overtook his body and once it reached his head, all feeling was lost. The only reaction at that point is to forfeit control of your body, and that's what happened to him. I saw him fall on the driveway, but there was nothing I could do.

The ambulance had been called and were on their way as my mom sat on a chair inside the house holding me in her lap, rocking me back and forth with a confident smile saying, "You will live and not die, you will live and not die, you will live and not die!" She repeated this over and over until it began to sound like a lullaby in my ears. This was one of the most tangible examples of faith that I had ever witnessed in my life. Faith, according to the Holy Bible, is defined as the substance of things hoped for and the evidence of things not yet seen. I had heard that many times before, but I had never seen it put to action quite like this. There was absolutely no evidence of any hope of survival or any sign of life for me. On the contrary, there was a lot of blood; my body got heavier and heavier and I could no longer support my own weight as my eyelids began getting closer and closer together. Despite all of these signs, my mom seemed almost completely unshaken. It was an amazing sight. This kind of faith would

eventually set a foundation for me in life and in business as it taught me that I'm not supposed to see things to believe it. I could actually believe to see it and that is what would make it materialize and that is how faith works. Wow!
I finally learned what faith is, although maybe a little too late as I was just about to give up.

This was it. Even I knew at this point that it would all soon be over. I felt excruciating pain but I didn't have the strength to fight through it. Even the small gasps of air had died down at this point. Chad who had somehow gathered himself together stood near by with his hands over his mouth panting hard saying "Oh my God, what's going on?" and my sister and my dad stood by the opened door waiting for the paramedics.
The final thoughts that ran through my head sounded like a poem in my spirit. Here's what it read:

Goodbye life, It was quite the adventure. I had the chance to be apart of a loving family who did their best to care for me and to raise me in the right way. Goodbye life, I hope I was a true friend to those who will remember me as one. Goodbye life, I hope the words of the last song I wrote paint an accurate picture of who I was, or who I was trying to become. Goodbye life, if I'm honest with myself, I know I didn't leave the most positive impact behind, but maybe this outcome will help someone else pick up where I left off. Goodbye life, I wish I got to know more about God and who Jesus Christ really is, because I feel like my life would have been better. Why 21,life? There were no signs, no hints, and no clues to alert me that this was where my journey would end. It felt so short, so unfulfilled. Goodbye life.

At that moment, I faintly looked at my mom and with a soft whisper said, "Mom I can't breathe anymore."
There was a millisecond of silence
"SHUT UP!" She yelled back at me.
What!? Suddenly my eyes sprung open! Her response sent my body into a quick shock that literally felt like she spoke life back into me. Her faith was seriously being put to the test but she was not backing down. This gave me a newfound inner strength. My mom seemed as if she was in

HOW?

another world as she began to repeat, "Jesus, Jesus, Jesus, Jesus", while rocking me back and forth. She was definitely seeing something, or more like someone that I wasn't. Jesus had to have been there assuring my mom that I was going to be ok, because that kind of confidence had no pretending in it at all. All this was too much for Chad as I saw him lose consciousness two more times and fall to the ground. Finally, the sound of the ambulance could be heard in the distance. They got louder and louder as they got closer and closer and hope began to sprout in my heart. The paramedics and several police officers raced up our front steps into the house and began doing what they're best at. The paramedics immediately held me and started removing the blood stained blankets to get a better understanding of where I had been cut, meanwhile the police officers tried to calm my parents down and assure them that everything was going to be ok. I'm pretty sure an officer had to rush to Chad's aid as well as he was completely out of it. During all of this, my mom continued speaking the name of Jesus repeatedly and as one of the officers tried to notion her that she could stop and that everything would be OK, my mom simply replied "*I'm talking to my God!*" and the officer backed off.

In no time at all, the paramedics had completed their initial observation and they rolled in a stretcher bed and very carefully lifted me up and placed me on it and loaded me into the ambulance. The last person I saw was my dad who held the ambulance door and looked me in the eyes and said," Dan, be strong! You're going to make it! We need you!" There he stood. My true best friend. The person who always believed in me and always supported me. My most trusted advisor, who I wished I had listened to more. My coach, my father and my pastor. As I briefly saw him standing at the ambulance door I remembered the track and field days and how he would always wait at the finish line for me at my track meets. Once I knew my dad was there, I would run my fastest to make him proud when I won. Many memories flashed before me as I watched the ambulance door close with my dad standing there and just like my first day of school, I stared into his face. He had that same look, those same eyes. It was then that I decided in myself that I am going to treat this circumstance like the biggest race of my life and I'm going to win. I'm going to make both of my parents proud. From that moment, no matter how great the temptation, I refused to close my eyes.

RENATA

A lot of what I do in business is simply a result of what I've experienced in my life. By now you understand that I was not very academically inclined and college and university were strangers to me. My teacher was good ol' life. Life is like an award-winning professor, teaching you lessons that you can't ignore, and placing you in situations you can't just simply get around and that kind of teaching has stuck with me. The lessons of life evolved out of everyday breathing, observing, doing, not doing, hearing, asking, climbing, and falling. It's just one big unforgettable lesson.

After the ambulance sirens had died down, I had to be airlifted and rerouted to St Michael's Hospital. It was a very intense ride. At higher altitudes, air is obviously much colder than on the ground, so needless to say I was freezing. The paramedics covered me in a blanket, but my body was already so weak at this point that I felt like I was feeling the freezing air directly on my skin. My open wounds were now covered in bloody bandages and the struggle to breathe was still there. Every time I would try and breathe it felt like the breath was leaving out of all the open cuts on my body. Every breath felt like I had bubbles in my lungs, and the pain, to say the least, was excruciating. The helicopter sound was ferociously loud as the propellers would beat against the wind. There was a small window to my right that I could see out of. It was now nighttime and for a tiny moment as I looked out and saw all the beautiful city lights and the massive CN tower, I thought in myself "Wow, what a beautiful night."

After we landed, the heavy beating of the helicopter vanished. Warmth began to slowly return to my body. The echoes of encouraging words coming from the coaching paramedics who were monitoring me ceased, and there was a moment of darkness. I call this moment the in-between. Whether I was dead, unconscious or seriously drugged, I didn't know, but after what felt like hours of torture, I found some peace. Thankfully, I had miraculously survived, as I became more and more aware of my surroundings and I regained a small degree of consciousness, in what was actually a very deep sleep. Slowly my eyes began to see light, but no tunnel this time. This felt like I was waking up from the craziest nightmare and for some reason I felt light headed and spaced out. When my eyes had fully opened, I saw Renata.

Renata was my understanding girlfriend. She had been my official girlfriend for one year, which in my twenty-one year old mind was the equivalent of ten years of marriage. I can imagine that by now she had pretty much gone through the same kind of torment that I did, but emotionally, which can be equally as damaging. I kept blinking because the morphine that the nurses had me hooked up to made my eyes glossy and it was difficult to see. Once I had blinked enough to create a sense of clarity, I looked Renata in her eyes and we just stared at each other for a minute or two without saying any words. I couldn't help but to peer into her light brown eyes and see if I could feel what she was feeling and to try and offer her a sense of comfort, but instead I ended up going farther than I had anticipated. I was immediately taken back to

HOW?

where we first met.

The Grade 3 school year had just begun and I was starting out in a brand new school. Clark Boulevard seemed like a nice school from the exterior and it had a nice little sandbox where I could already see myself parading around once I made new friends and established some popularity. I knew I could do it, but it would take some time and some class clowning to make it happen. As I arrived on my first day, I remember one of the office secretaries escorting me to my classroom where I would meet my new teacher, Mrs. Finkle. Dang! It's a portable. I hated portables, mainly because, well, let's just say everything you've ever heard about Canadian weather is true.

I walked up the wooden steps opened the door and stepped into the class room as all twenty mini heads including Mrs. Finkle's turned to look at me, the new kid. I could feel every single student making his or her judgments, assumptions and conclusions about me but that was normal and it didn't phase my young mind much. As Mrs. Finkle got up to greet me and introduce me to the class, that's when I saw her. She had beautiful, long, golden hair, explosive eyes and a light purple Beauty and the Beast sweater. I was in kid-love! She looked at me for half a second, and unimpressed she continued doodling in her pastel colored notebook. I remember thinking she looked like Goldilocks but this was no fairytale storybook. She was real and I had to get to know her!

As days went by, I very subtly started introducing my "class clownism" anytime an opportunity had presented itself. Mrs. Finkle was infamous for math flash cards. She loved them and she must of thought that the entire class did too. She would hold up various math equations and the first person to answer the problem correctly would receive a sticker or a pencil at the end of class. I would always shoot my hand up whether I knew the answer or not as it was the perfect time to fire some kind of joke to send the class into laughter. As usual, it worked. Weeks went by and I had comfortably earned my position as one of the most popular kids in the class, and after a few months, it was safe to say I was one of the most popular kids in the school. All the little girls liked me because I was always trying to make them laugh and I was very outspoken. I wasn't afraid to embarrass myself, doing strange and unordinary things like dressing up as a Spice Girl and performing 'Spice Up Your Life' at the school talent show. Impersonating pop star Aqua and creating my rendition of *Barbie Girl* was the icing on the cake. Teachers loved me, girls loved me and even the lunch teachers and crossing guards heard many interesting things about me. I was officially "The Grade Three King Of Clark." But, still no Renata. Renata was the type of girl who hated when guys liked her. I used to send notes to her friends in class and at recess professing my infatuation for the young Goldilocks. Let's just say the notes I received back didn't exactly set the stage for a fairytale ending. One day in class I told her I wanted her to be my girlfriend and she responded by using her fist to splash my lunch milk packet in my face. Either her Goldilocks image was a gimmick or she found me very annoying. When it comes to challenges in life whether business, work or love, I was never one to back down easily. I have always believed that if something were hard to attain, then once I achieved it, it would be well worth the fight. I know what you're probably thinking.

These are pretty serious feelings for an eight-year-old boy.
Well, what can I say? It was love at first sight!
My persistence had began to prevail as rumours started going around the school that Renata actually liked me and this made school very interesting for me.
Was she playing hard to get the entire time?
Was she jealous of all the other girls I was spending my recess with?

HOW?

Whatever it was, I wasn't going to waste any time. I had to find out! One day as we were all enjoying some free time in Mrs. Finkle's class, I decided to take a piece of paper, crumple it together and form a paper ring. I steadfastly decided that I was going to just try my luck, and propose to Renata right in the middle of the class. Now, I knew, this was going to go one of two ways. Either Goldilocks falls in love with my wittiness and perseverance, and marries me, and I buy her a horse and ride off into the sunset. Or she gets embarrassed, hates me all the more and finds a bag of milk to throw in my face. It was a risk I was willing to take. I got down on one knee at her desk and with hopeful, endearing eyes and said, "Renata, will you marry me?"

She blinked. I blinked.

She blushed.

"Ewww!! Get away from me!!" She was totally embarrassed.

Folks, I failed.

Or had I? My persistence was pretty relentless. At 8 years old, why wouldn't it be? After a few more months of perfecting how to make her laugh, Goldilocks gave in, and became my new girlfriend. Renata thinks this is the part of our story that I tend to exaggerate about, but that's what makes it our story, from my perspective, not hers (*chuckle chuckle*). I think I must have really embarrassed her when she turned me down before, because at this point she really liked me a lot. At this age it was more of a great friendship, but in my eyes we were in love. We would talk on the phone, spend our recess together, write notes to each other and everyday after school my dad would wait for me, as I would walk Renata to her mother in her yellow Toyota and send her off.

My nightmare came true at the end of grade three, when Renata broke the news to me that her parents were moving to another part of the city and thus she was forced to leave Clark Boulevard and attend a new school. Our little hearts were broken. My Goldilocks that I had worked so hard for was moving away. When the day came and Renata had moved away, I was distraught. We would still call each other to talk about whatever 8 year olds talk about, but eventually, we lost contact and sadly our friendship withered away.

I graduated from Clark Boulevard, moved on to middle school and years had gone by since I spoke or even saw Renata. As time passed by, she started to become more of a childhood memory, but never forgotten. One day I remember I bumped into an old mutual friend from Clark Boulevard School in the shopping mall who just so happened to have recently reconnected with Renata. After catching up with this old school mate, she was kind enough to bridge the connection between Renata and myself and after a few phone calls; we set up a date to reunite.

Seeing Renata again was a dream come true. She was no less beautiful and still maintained that Goldilocks hair that I loved. Unfortunately, we lived so far apart and we were still so young that even with our new reconnection, it was nearly impossible to stay in touch. Once again we faded away. It wasn't until my early teenage years that I caught another quick glimpse of Renata as I was leaving out of an all ages club called Club 108. I was with some of my friends exiting the party when a girl with black hair standing off to the side confronted me saying, "Omg! Danny? Are you Danny Lewis from Clark?" Astonished and confused at first, I thought this was just a groupie who probably heard of me from somewhere and had a major crush on me or something, but after an in-depth look, sure enough, it was Renata. We were worlds apart by now as I was just at the early stages of my fashion dreams and Renata seemed to have reinvented her self as well. Goldilocks with black hair? This was not the fairytale I knew. We didn't really stop to catch up and maybe I thought I was too cool for Renata now or maybe she had

HOW?

forgotten who we used to be to each other. Whatever it was, it ended quickly as I confirmed it was me, acknowledged that I knew it was her, smiled and we continued walking in our own directions.

The year 2007 rolled around and like most people I had just jumped on the new Facebook wagon. It was the first social media platform of its kind. An MSN Messenger on steroids, if you will. Once I moved up the ranks and surpassed the novice stage of a Facebook user, I began using Facebook to try and locate past friends and family by entering their names in the search tool and scoping through the many results that would pop up in hopes of seeing a familiar face in the profile picture. Contrary to our last run in, Renata had always been someone I was interested in connecting with. She however, was next to impossible to find on Facebook. For some reason, I came up with the idea that her last name was Diaz, so I would search for Renata Diaz to no avail. Coincidentally Renata shared with me that she was also searching for me on Facebook and friend-by-friend we were getting closer and closer to finding each other electronically until that special day when the notification finally popped up.

1 New Message Sender: Renata Lopez.

The message read: Is this Danny Lewis from Clark Boulevard?

I was so taken back I immediately clicked over to her photos to begin looking through her life and her past. *What was she doing now? Did she have a boyfriend? What school did she go to?* I wanted to know everything about my long lost childhood sweetheart, Renata.

Luckily the timing was perfect! Renata had just recently gone through a breakup, and although a little heartbroken, she was ready to move on.

(Insert Daniel here)

After a few chats back and forth on the phone and via Facebook, Renata and I decided we would meet up for an appetizer at Boston Pizza. I must admit I was just a tad bit nervous. It had been years since we had seen each other. We were nineteen now and surely we were different people. Would we still be able to actually connect? Was it going to be awkward?

When I drove onto Renata's street I pulled up to the stop sign and patiently waited. Eventually I saw a girl walking just a few meters away from the car in grey jogging pants and a long coat. Her hair was still black and very curly and she carried nothing with her as she tucked her hands in her jacket pockets to keep them warm. As she approached the front end of my red Integra, the headlights put her into full perspective. She smiled, reached for the passenger door and sat down inside my car. "OMG! It's you, Danny!" she shouted, as we kind of giggled at the irony of what seemed to be fate and destiny at work. We arrived to Boston Pizza, took off our coats, ordered our food and it began. We spent two hours catching up and pouring our entire life out to each other, both the good and the bad. We were both so open and so comfortable that you would never think it had been years since we had last spoke. After lots of laughs, and lots of pasta we decided that maybe we should both get home. After all, it was getting late. I waved down our server to ask for the bill while Renata and I reflected on the awesome night we had so far and shared our excitement about how we should do this more often. As the bill came, I gave it a quick glance and realized maybe I had too much fun, forgetting how expensive dining out could be. I remained very casual but I had no idea what my account balance was. I asked for the debit machine thinking to myself " What am I doing!" The server brought the unit and I swiped. *Insufficient funds.* I instantly started sweating under my arms but I played it cool and did the old "let me try that again" tactic to pretend that something had to be wrong with their machine. It declined again. Renata didn't bring a purse or her wallet so instead of rambling through her pockets to give me any kind of hope, she just gave me a curious look and shrugged her shoulders with her palms facing up as to say "Well, what do we do now?" I politely asked the server to give us a second, as my mind quickly scrambled for ideas on how to get myself out of this situation and get this bill paid. I know I couldn't call Jon because he would be out late somewhere downtown with his friends. Chad was probably at work. My last resort was Tay. I dialed his number and when he answered I begged him to rush over to Boston Pizza and bring me some money to pay this bill. Being the loyal friend he was, he quickly responded with "I'm on my way!" This whole situation really sucked and taught me a lot about first impressions, but there was nothing I could do at this point to change mine. After I hung up the phone and told Renata the solution I had put in place, she looked at me for a good five seconds and I looked back at her as we burst into an unquenchable laughter.

Let's face it, fate kept presenting opportunities for Renata and I to just grab love by the horns, but circumstances would always separate us. I lost her 3 times and I wasn't willing to let Goldilocks slip away this time. If she could stick with me through a first date that I publicly couldn't afford and simply laugh it off, why shouldn't we just turn life into one big adventure and laugh our way through it all. Renata and I started dating a few days later and we've never spent one day apart ever since.

"Dan? Are you ok?" Renata said with a small empathetic voice.

"Yes." I replied. "What happened?"

Renata gave me the very brief edited version of what she knew about the situation, as she didn't want me focusing on any traumatic thoughts while I should have been resting. Jonathan stood beside Renata and immediately burst into tears. I thought of the A.J incident when we were kids, and how much Jonathan wished he could have been there for me now like he was back then. Jon promised me that he was going to find out who did this to me and that each and every one of them would pay for what they had done. I extended my hand out to my brother and he came close and held it. I understood his desire for revenge. Jon was my defender when I couldn't defend myself. But this was no A.J situation. This couldn't be fixed with a simple punch. I knew that taking care of this type of situation was like playing with life and death. I looked him straight in his eyes as I tried to muster up enough strength to speak a few words and I said, "Don't revenge. Just let God take care of it." Though drawn back at my reply, I'm sure the thoughts of almost losing a brother, and then seeing him survive, helped him understand my perspective to just try and keep the peace. That night a major change happened in me, and the extent of that change I was yet to find out. Only God could have given me a second chance at life.

The name Renata comes from the Latin word 'Renatus' which in short is translated as 'rebirth', 'reborn' or 'born again.' When I think about the significance of Renata in my life from my childhood in Mrs. Finkle's class all the way up until that moment where she stood by my bedside in the hospital, there could have been no one more fitting to stand next to me as my rebirth began to take place. I was like a caterpillar who by reason of life's circumstances was wrapped away inside a cocoon of mystery. What would happen after all this? Who will I be now? Only the process of time could show who would come bursting out of that cocoon with a new understanding, purpose and new goals. This was a transformation shared and encouraged by my lovely girlfriend, and now wife, Renata.

I PROMISE

My hospital experience was one of the greatest moments of self-reflection that I have ever had in my life. I felt as if something in my eyes literally transformed and now I was seeing life in a whole new way. I had many different tubes and needles hooked up to my body so I spent most of my time in the hospital bed. Renata stayed with me in the hospital the entire five days I was checked in, only going home once for a few hours to take a shower and get some food. I watched Renata, as she would ask the nurse to allow her to wash my feet and lightly bathe me to give me some form of a shower. She brushed my teeth, she fed me, and she even helped me relearn how to walk. When nighttime would come, she would leave my room to go and sleep on one of the couches in the lounge. One night she snuck into my hospital room to watch a movie with me on the small overhead TV. She cared about me so much, and I appreciated her so much. One night I sat up in my bed and looked at Renata as she slept curled up in a fetal position on the chair in my room, and I made a promise. I promised myself as soon as I got out of this hospital bed and my wounds were healed, I was going to marry Renata, or propose to her at least. She had unintentionally proven that she could be with me in the worst of times and the best of times and that's all I needed to know. She was willing to give everything up for me and

I was willing to do the same and more for her.

Renata wasn't the only person I was watching in the hospital. I watched the nurses, the doctors, the other patients, and the families of those patients visiting them. I watched the police officers, I watched my family and friends visit me, I watched the custodial staff cleaning the hallways; everything and everyone stood out to me. I felt like God had given me a new pair of HD eyes and now I was able to look into everything in a different way. I had many deep thoughts about life and people and myself and my past. I asked myself a question inside, "Dan, if you would have died, what kind of impact did you leave behind in this world and in people's lives? How would you be remembered? What did you accomplish?" A sense of purpose began to boil inside of me as I realized that my answer to these questions were not very satisfying. Immediately, motivation started to give birth in me and the will to do good and evoke positive change in people's lives started to awake inside. A desire to establish a true relationship with Jesus Christ erupted in my spirit. Forgiveness towards the guy that stabbed me bubbled inside my heart. Everything around me looked different and I started to become really excited about living. I couldn't wait to get back on my feet and step out into the world and explore this new me. I felt like a kid with a new bike that couldn't wait to take it for a ride and experiment with the gears and the brakes to see how fast and how far I could actually go. I started creating all these promises to myself. I promised that I was going to cherish every second of life that I was granted, I would do my best to see the best in others and I promised to break through every barrier that tried to hold me back from fulfilling these promises. Introducing the new Daniel.

After five long days in the hospital I finally got back on my two feet. With my new perspective on life, I was ready to live life to the fullest and put my whole heart in everything that I was going to do going forward. The first thing I wanted to do was marry Renata. I wanted to propose to her to show her my commitment and my appreciation for her after everything we had experienced together. I also wanted to build a stronger relationship with my parents. After all, they saved my life, and they had always been there for me. My parents lived trustworthy lives and I decided that in all my decisions, I would always consult with them first. So one day, a few months after the stabbing, I sat down and asked them what their thoughts were on me getting engaged. They were totally for it. Having been married themselves for over twenty-four years; they had shared a beautiful and happy marriage and wanted the same for my siblings and me. With their OK, I managed to scrape up a little bit of money and I purchased an engagement ring. I tried to find something unique that would symbolize our growing friendship and I found a gold ring that was formed into a rose. It was perfect. I had it all planned out, and for the first time in my life, I was very nervous.

I took Renata to a lake where we both just sat and talked about life, like we always did. I felt like I kept mumbling my words and not making any sense. Wow! Those guys in the movies made it look so easy, but in real life this was a very different experience. Somehow I finally found the courage mid way through our little date to drop down on one knee and pull out the ring.

"Will you marry me!?"

A million questions popped into my head. "What if she says no? Are we too young to do this? Will she like the ring? Why am I so nervous?"

"YESSSSSSSSS!"

Renata shouted as she began to jump up and down! She started running around, and then she came back and gave me a big hug. No tears, no awkward moments. Just a whole lot of smiles, jumping and running.

Well, that definitely went better than the first time I tried it in Mrs. Finkle's class.

We chose the date June 5th, 2010, a year after I proposed. Let the wedding planning begin.

It's amazing how quickly time flies when you are planning a wedding. I mean, one year sounds like a long time, but in fact, it actually felt like a matter of minutes! As time passed, my life continued to transform. I was engaged and a newly committed Christian with many goals that I now wanted to accomplish. Most of the stab wounds on my body were healed, but not without some complications. The cut to my neck seriously damaged my nerves leaving the entire left side of my face and neck with a tingling numbness anytime my face was touched. The gash in my abdomen was very deep and had somehow managed to get infected creating a big bubble inside of the wound. This bubble immediately had to be removed and a home nurse was assigned to come to my house once a week to open the wound, clean it and redress it. It was so painful and I always dreaded the moment when I heard her voice at the front door. Apart from the dreadful, excruciating pain, I did, however, become very appreciative of the tedious work that nurses do for people who are unable to help themselves. I don't think I really ever considered what my mom actually did for a living until now. My mom dedicated her whole life to taking care of the elderly, but this was so much more than a career for her. This was her calling. Every now and then when we were kids, my mom would always bring my brother and I to meet her patients at their homes or in the hospital and sometimes she would bring her patients with us to go out and grab a bite to eat. She cared about each and every one of her patients and always showed them the utmost care. When their families couldn't be there for them especially during the holidays, my mom was there for them, just like how these nurses were there for me.

After weeks and weeks of the nurse taking care of me and nursing my wound, the gash began to heal properly and close up but not without leaving a big, dark scar, even

HOW?

to this day. I have a total of five scars from the incident and operation that look at me every time I stand in the mirror after a shower. These scars remind me of the amazing dedication and precision that doctors, nurses and all medical professionals put into their work everyday all around the world. When I thought about the paramedics that rushed to my house that day and the police officers that responded to the call, I made another promise. I promised that one day I was going to find someway of thanking all these everyday heroes. Not just because of what they did for me, but because of what they do for people all over the world, everyday. When a call comes in to the police or the firefighters or the paramedics, they don't ask what the colour, social status or the net worth of the victim. They just come. These are true heroes and I wanted to do something to honour them.

Every April 14th, on the anniversary of my traumatic experience, my company T By Daniel now invites all paramedics, doctors, nurses, police officers, nursing assistants, and basically anyone in the medical or law enforcement industry to come into our tea shop and enjoy a free cup of tea. I also try to make sure that I'm personally there to shake their hand, thank them and even pose for a picture to let our customers know who these awesome individuals are. When I'm driving on the road now and I see ambulance lights in my rearview mirror, I make it my duty to pull over quickly and safely to allow them to easily pass by and get to where they're going promptly. I've been that person that they're trying to get to and I've learned that every second counts. I promised myself that I would always maintain a sense of giving back whether in the form of respect that is due, a kind gesture, or a small gift. After all, it's the little things that count.

As a motivational keynote speaker, I frequently get asked to speak to aspiring entrepreneurs and business students who are eager to enter into the marketplace. The most popular question I always get asked is "How do you stay motivated in your business?" There is no easy answer to this question. Every person is motivated by different things, and what motivates me may not be what motivates the people listening to me. However, I always tell them the truth. My answer is simply my mission. When I need to find that push or get that entrepreneurial fire to ignite in me, I stop and ask myself: Why am I doing this? What am I trying to accomplish? Is it clearly defined? Is it rewarding? I was so close to losing my life. Because of this, my business has always been about so much more than just making money, marketing strategies and consumer trends. My goal is to make everyday count and to make the people I encounter feel as special as they are. There is only one me, and only one you. If we cross paths, I want you to understand that the world wouldn't be same without you.

Sound corny? Perhaps. But when life is slipping away from you, all you think about is how much you wish you would have been kinder, more loving and let the people you loved know how much you love them.

So what's the take home here?

Well based on my own personal experiences I would say, whatever you do in life, whether it's business, family, or work related, do it for more than money or personal satisfaction. Money comes and goes and personal satisfaction changes as you change. Plus, we're not here forever, so if your goal is to only satisfy yourself then that goal will leave with you.

I often use an analogy when I speak to aspiring entrepreneurs, who dream of making millions running their own business, and quit working for other people. There's nothing wrong with making millions and working for yourself, but when considering business try to think of it like this: Business is like a car, and fuel or gas is like money. You obviously need fuel to drive your car, just like you need money to operate a business. After all, it's the gas that will allow that car to take you on a journey, help you to pick up your friends, or allow you to take those solo rides out in the evening as the sun sets. But no one ever buys a car based on his or her excitement to put gas in it. I mean, just think about it. Imagine yourself driving off in your new car, heading into the gas station with the biggest smile on your face, and getting excited at the thought of Octane 94 vs. Octane 83. Picture yourself jumping up and down as you pump that gas in your new car, calling all your friends and telling them "Guess what grade diesel I'm using!"

Pretty weird, right?

Well it's exactly the same when people get excited about money. As important as it may seem, money is just the fuel you need to assist you along life's many adventures. Without it, life is certainly harder. But having it, doesn't necessarily make life easier.

I'll leave you with this amazing statement that my father taught me about riches.

One day in church, my dad asked the congregation;

"Who is a rich person?"

We all sat around, trying to come up with the deepest answer we could think of. But the word rich had always seemed to go hand and hand with money. Until my dad shattered that thought for me, forever.

My dad looked at us all and said "You know who a rich person is? A rich person is a person with a keen sense of responsibility, and a high regard for human life." Wow! In other words, don't spend your life being excited about the fuel. Get out there, live and love because our days are not promised and the end of life has caught many people off guard.

On a side note, all this talk about fuel has my tummy grumbling. Pizza, anyone?

KNOCK-KNOCK
(THE DOMINO EFFECT)

Newly engaged and refocused once again, I decided to start making my way back into the work force. I didn't just want a general labour job or a beginner restaurant position. I wanted something that offered a little more growth and stability, something that could actually sustain me and my soon to be wife. I decided to go where all the cool kids go to look for jobs.
Craigslist!

If you know anything about job search sites like Craigslist, then you know that the majority of the job postings you find are pretty much dead end jobs, scams or high-paying positions that require you to move to space to get there. Even though there were a million and one reasons not to look on a job search site for a real job, when you're ready to get working you'll look just about anywhere. One day I noticed a job posting on Craigslist that read: LOOKING TO HIRE A MANAGER INTERESTED IN BECOMING A PIZZA FRANCHISEE! My first thought was... Huh? Pizza? Then I clicked the link and continued to read the job posting to

HOW?

see if this was a real job offer to work at a pizza shop or if it was a subliminal street drug recruitment post. The post ended with an invite for interested applicants to call a Werner at the listed phone number or to visit the store address. I figured I have nothing to lose so why not call and see what happens.

"Thank you for choosing Yummy's Pizza. Ryan speaking, how can I help you?" I thought to myself, this guy sounds far too polite to be a drug dealer, so this job posting must be real!

I expressed my interest in finding out more about the job offer and Ryan notified me that Werner, the owner wasn't in, but I could call back or drop by sometime the next morning. So the next day I saddled my horse a.k.a my car and took a drive down to see if I could maybe meet with Werner or at least drop my resume off. I found the shop, parked, walked inside and immediately started mind drooling from the delicious aroma of baked pizza crust that filled my nostrils. I decided that whether or not I met Werner, I was definitely going to treat myself to a pizza. As soon as I walked into the tiny pizza shop, I saw a young, freckled face man pop his head from behind a tiled wall, covered in cornmeal and flour. He smiled and greeted me saying, "Welcome to Yummy's Pizza, I'll be with you in one minute." I thanked the pizza maker and took a step back to observe the shop and all that was going on. I couldn't help but notice what appeared to be hundreds and hundreds of folded pizza boxes stacked all over the counters and shelves and racks. With that many boxes already folded, they must have sold a lot of pizzas. The young pizza maker was zipping across the production line; rolling, slapping, tossing and saucing pizzas in a way that I never thought was possible. He finished up and returned to the counter literally in less than a minute.
"Hey, how can I help you?"

It was obvious that he was the only person in the shop as there was no one else behind the counter with

him. The young man was probably a part-time university student working the morning shift. I figured that Werner wasn't around so maybe I should just leave my resume with him. I told him that I came in hopes to meet Werner in regards to the manager job offering I saw on Craigslist.
"Oh, okay well I'm Werner." He responded.
Huhhhhh?
How?
Really?

Those were the first words that echoed in my head. I was completely thrown off by how young Werner looked. For a split second I thought to myself, isn't Werner the owner? How could he be so young and already own a pizza shop? That's crazy! I was expecting a much older guy, not covered in flour and certainly not making pizzas. After I recovered from feeling stupid at the narrow-minded assumptions that I had made, I formally introduced myself and expressed my interest in the franchisee in training position. Werner looked really busy, but he quickly stated that if I were able to hang around for the next thirty minutes, he would finish making some large pizza orders and then interview me on the spot.

#Unexpected. Having no job, no money and a wedding coming soon I quickly agreed, as he quickly jumped back behind the wall to bang out some more pizzas. Time passed and eventually Werner washed up his hands and came out to the front to meet with me and ask me a few questions. I can't recall exactly how our conversation went, but I'm sure it was something like this:
"Ever made a pizza in your life?"
"Nope." I replied.
What's your availability like?
"I'm completely open and hoping!"
"How'd you hear about the job offer?"
"Craigslist, which by the way really surprises me."
We chuckled, we talked and he explained to me exactly what he was looking for. Werner needed a long-term hire

with the vision of running their own shop and finding a motivated team to make it happen. I loved it! He was so energetic, focused and had a clear vision of what he wanted, plus he looked super-duper young, which was quite inspiring. After we finished speaking, he immediately notified me that he would pass along my information to his partners and give me a call to setup a second interview. YES! I guess I must have said something he liked for him to invite me back. There was hope for me.

A few days later, Werner and his two partners, one of whom was his dad, scheduled me to come in for a second interview at a neighbouring restaurant. When I arrived, the three gentlemen were just heading into the restaurant and the eldest of the three, held the door open for me as I walked up to the restaurant. When I was a couple feet away the gentleman said to me, "With that kind of walk, we could just skip the interview and hire you!" He was obviously joking, but aside from that comfortable icebreaker and his extended hand with a firm warm handshake, I could already tell that this man was really keen on the personality of a potential hire. I giggled and then shook his hand as he introduced himself to me, "Nice to meet you, I'm Werner."

Huh? I thought the young freckled face pizza maker guy was Werner. With a twisted face of confusion the older Werner knew exactly what I was thinking. He quickly informed me that the young freckled Werner was his son, a junior. Ohhhh! I get it now. They were both named Werner, father and son. The third gentleman was Shane, a "graduate" from the franchisee in training program, who was already operating his own location. We all sat down over coffee as they began to explain the long history of who they are, how they got here and where they're heading. Due to the very recent tragedy I had just come out of, it only seemed right for me to briefly explain what happened, who I was, how I ended up here and why there was a huge protruding scar on my neck. This conversation eventually led us into discussing our faith and it turned out that we were both Christians and had a lot in common in regards to our beliefs. An hour went by and I already felt like I was a part of the family. To make a long story short, the second interview went well. They felt I was a good fit, and Daniel was officially the new Yummy's Pizza Manager and franchisee in training with new sights set on one day opening my very own pizza shop.

The skills that I was able to learn during my time at Yummy's theoretically could have paved the way for me to start any kind of business. Although I was hired as a manger, I was still privileged enough to get a taste of every single aspect of the pizza business. This means I went from pizza delivery guy to pizza maker to general manager all while fulfilling the role of a franchisee in training. One of the hardest challenges of being hired as a manager, as opposed to starting from the bottom and working your way up, is convincing your crew that you are capable of a management role, even though you technically have much less practical experience than they do. I remember my first couple of weeks on the job and how dumb I felt every time one of the part-time school kids would try to hide their frustration at my failed attempts of making a sellable pizza. In my head I kept thinking, "C'mon Dan, it's just a pizza you can do this!" Four minutes later I was just sprinkling the final curds of cheese on a perfect Meatzza Feast pizza.

You're probably thinking, "So... what's the big deal? Four minutes is not that bad." Now is probably a good time for me to mention that as a manager I was expected to make a pizza from a raw dough ball to loading it in the oven in 45 seconds... Yeah, no kidding, right? How was I ever going to earn the respect of the employees that I manage if they see me as a failure from the jump start and they are all ten times better than me? This was like mission impossible and I was certainly no Tom Cruise.

Weeks went by and I would show up for my shifts

everyday, learning about everything that goes into running a top performing pizza shop. I learned about how to properly store raw dough and how to properly temper the dough so that it has the perfect rise once baked. I learned how to stock, enter, order and monitor inventory. I learned how to cut and box pizzas, answer phones, take orders, run deliveries and open and close the store. Little by little I was becoming one 'spicy pepperoni!'

As spicy as I was becoming, there was still one huge problem; I couldn't make a 45 second pizza. To further validate as to why this was so important for me to be able to do, please allow me to teleport you to any given Friday evening at Yummy's Pizza. Imagine orders upon orders of pizzas left, right and center, from hungry patrons who all seemed to agree that there is no better dinner solution on a Friday night than to grab delicious pizza. Werner had notified me that it would be impossible for me to manage a Friday evening shift unless I could make fast pizzas because if worse came to worse and the employees started falling behind on the screen orders, the manager would have to jump onto the line and really turn things up a notch. This was why it was extremely important that I put the pedal to the metal.

I'm a strong believer in practicing and working hard at something until you get it, whether that means starting a business, growing a business or even making a pizza in 45 seconds. I was so eager to get my pizza making time up to par, that I would study how all the other managers did it and then simply ask them to time me with a stop watch so I could track and make note of my improvement. As time went on, I continued to time and track my progress, until one special day eventually I did it! I actually managed to get my pizza time down to 45 seconds. I never thought that making a pizza could ever be so rewarding.

Werner would always pull out his stopwatch during slower times to check up on our times and to ensure none of us were getting rusty. This consistent maintenance helped keep the store upkeep, and also kept the staff including me in tip top shape.

Every time I would make pizzas, my body had this strange reaction where I would naturally bounce up and down, wiggling my hips as I beat away on the dough. It was a habit that I was always made fun of for but hey, it helped me to make pizzas faster so I stuck with it. With fast pizza making now under my belt, I was able to comfortably re-focus my attention on actually managing the store and growing in other areas of my management role. The employees started trusting me and building a fun relationship with me in the store. Thus was the beginning of the glory days at Yummy's Pizza. I just had to share my newfound excitement and this wonderful opportunity with Chad. I thought, we've always done everything together, and that maybe he too could benefit from joining the franchisee in training program. I explained to him how it all worked, the opportunity that was at hand, and that maybe; just maybe, this was the break that we had been so desperately looking for since our high school days. Chad gave it some thought, and as always he was on board. I introduced him to little Werner, big Werner and Shane. It was gold! They loved Chad too, and were willing to train him to open up his location as well! Could things get any better than this? Chad and I would have our own franchises in the same company. It seemed like nothing in life could ever separate us.

I DO

My training at Yummy's lasted months, but with much dedication, both on my part and Werner's part, we were able to create a pretty decent general manager out of me. Life was piecing itself together better than I could have ever imagined. Whoever thought I would have landed myself the opportunity to franchise my own store, at just twenty-two years old. I was thrilled. Not only had I landed myself a pretty sweet opportunity, I was also about to make the big switch from a single man into a married man. Although I was still young I was completely ready for all of these great new opportunities that were in the making.

The wedding planning months were fun. We had to go out and pick our colours, our invitations, our flowers and all those other little fine details. We also had to make the infamous guest list, which featured some of our all time and obvious favourites such as Chad, Jonathan and Tay. Renata and I also decided that we should invite Werner and his wife to our wedding because as time passed, they ended up becoming more like friends rather than just employers.

June 5, 2010 sped around the corner like a 100 meter

sprinter going for the gold. Before we blinked, it was actually our wedding day! Now, I know this is usually the part in the story where I would start telling you about how nervous I got and that I started breaking down and having cold feet about the whole wedding, but the truth was, I wasn't the least bit nervous. Obviously I was super excited that I was just about to seal the deal with the love of my life and my childhood sweetheart, but the thought of this made our wedding day all the more natural and special with a great anticipation to just get to the "I Do!" And begin our new lives together.

The weather forecast called for rain all week, and thus far it had not been wrong. This was slightly detrimental for us, as we had planned an outdoor wedding. But, just like a fairytale, the morning of June 5th was beaming rays of sunlight, and a beautiful warm breeze. I woke up with rays of sun blasting in my face and a big smile of excitement. I enjoyed my last breakfast at home with my family, laughing and getting ready for the big day. I proceeded to get dressed with my brother as my dad assisted me with my cuff links and pearl white suit. We chose green, white, and salmon as the colours for our garden themed summer wedding. At around 2:00 p.m., as the limo approached my parents' home to pick me up it finally hit me, like a hammer to the head. I, Daniel Lewis, was actually getting married, and the woman that would be walking down the aisle with me is my precious Renata, the grade three Goldilocks. Wow! Forget Beyoncé, I was feeling like the real Destiny's Child.

Another really special part about the events that were about to unfold was that my Dad, who was now an ordained Pastor, would be the officiator of our wedding ceremony and would actually sanction our marriage. Could it be any more magical than this?

We arrived at the garden green house, where the wedding ceremony would take place. Chad and my brother would be accompanying me to the altar, as my best man

HOW?

and groomsman. We hung around outside the green house for about ten minutes, taking pictures and hugging friends and family as we all began to make our way into the green house. Little by little, more and more people started to arrive until the green house was nearly at its capacity. As I looked out into the audience I saw Werner and his wife as he gave me a go-get-'em-tiger wink and a smile. I saw all the members of my old rap group. I saw acquaintances and old high school friends. As I observed the crowd so many memories crossed my mind and inside I thought to myself: man oh man, life is truly a beautiful thing.

I stood patiently at the altar, in my white suit. I was going through a phase of growing out my hair in a desperate attempt to resemble the Brazilian soccer player Ronaldinho. Let's just say, I came up really short, literally. If you don't know who Ronaldinho is, now would probably be a good time to Google him, just to better understand the look I was trying to go for. So, there I stood, white teeth, white suit, lime green vest and pocket square with my curly wet mop hairstyle, as Renata likes to call it. When I look back at our now privately secured and hidden away wedding pictures, I must admit, I kind of look like a black Side Show Bob from *The Simpsons*. Pretty scary. Conversations were happening all over the green house and in a sudden moment they turned into silence with faint 'oohs' and 'ahhs' especially at the back row. I came to the conclusion that my lovely bride had arrived. The wedding march music queued and the ceremony had now officially begun. I glanced over at Chadwin and my brother as the flower girls began to walk in showering people with peachy- green flower petals and awkward smiles. Ok fine, now I was officially a little bit nervous, just a little. What does she look like? Will she appreciate how I look? What if she pulls one of those Hollywood chick flick scenes and runs out of the ceremony crying "I can't do this!" What if somebody actually stands up and objects to our marriage when Pastor asks, "If anyone thinks we should not be together, please say so now." All these thoughts ran through my mind, but I also remembered that this woman was the same Renata who lay beside me in my toughest times. God knew exactly what he was doing. The music suddenly faded out and the official wedding song began to play. Step by step a beautiful, rosy-cheeked woman partially hidden by a white-laced veil began to walk down the aisle towards me. She looked at me and I could immediately tell that she was actually looking into me instead of at me. She never saw my hair or my fancy suit and I stopped looking at her pretty white dress, and together we met in a very secret place in our hearts where nobody was and nobody could see us. This was a special moment between my wife and I. As she joined me at the altar and we turned and faced each other, I could hear her heart asking me questions like, "Do you really love me?" "Are you nervous?" "Do you remember when we first met?" And inside my heart I would reply with the same answer over and over, "I am going to take care of you forever." The entire conversation between us was silent and translated into faint little smiles and giggles. Here we were. From school, to Facebook, to first dates, and heartbreaks, and now this moment. Pastor proceeded with the ceremony and the vows and the exchange of rings and prayer and we sealed the ceremony with a promise, all the I do's and a kiss. Goldilocks officially became Renata Lewis and I officially became her faithful husband.

As we left the green house and headed outside for pictures and meet and greets, I recall looking up in the sky and pondering at how beautiful and sunny the day turned out. There wasn't a cloud in sight. It was little instances like this that started to strengthen my faith in God. Whenever life had faced me with a situation that was beyond my control, God had always come through for me; even in the little things that I thought would not matter. Our wedding was what one would consider to be a small wedding? As we only invited 30-40 guests. Sadly, when I look back now at the guests that attended, I don't see a lot of people who genuinely cared about Renata and myself, but rather a lot of people who felt it was probably their duty to be there if they were going to continue to be called friends. The reception was held at my parents' house in their backyard. It was small and intimate but loaded with character. Luckily the rain continued to hold off so the evening was well underway. We ate a beautiful dinner, cut the cake and played a few games, as everyone was getting ready for all the grand speeches. Almost everybody was lined up to say something. My brother spoke, my friends spoke and of course Chad spoke. I guess I should have known what to expect from a guy who turned a frog in a novel into a story of "Hoppi-ness." My experiences with Chad were typically all of him saying the wrong things at the wrong times. As Chad began to express his appreciation for my friendship and his great experiences with Renata being my girlfriend and how he knew she was the one for me, he then went on to explain that he was always the third wheel on mine and Renata's dates and how annoyed he would get. Everyone chuckled at the cute stories and one would think that Chad stopped there. But not quite. He then went on to say that one night he was in the back seat of my car as I dropped Renata home and he explained to the entire guest list how gross it was to sit there and endure me kissing Renata goodbye. Great, thanks Chad, (very sarcastically.) No one had ever witnessed a purple human being until then. I was so embarrassed.

    Up next was Werner, and I figured this would be interesting. He introduced himself and began telling stories of my beginning struggles and challenges of working at Yummy's Pizza, and then proceeded to explain to the guests how he has never seen someone so determined, so enthusiastic and so willing to do what it takes to succeed like me. He concluded by saying to my wife Renata, that if I would be even half the husband to her that I am as a worker then she had just found herself quite the amazing husband. Wow! I was speechless and Renata was probably crying. It's the most amazing feeling to hear your employer stand up and tell your spouse how great of a person they think you are. It basically reassures your spouse that when they are not with you they are still giving it everything they've got. Thanks, Werner.

The night went on and the reception had been far spent. We had made plans for a limo to pick everyone up and drive us to a Spanish club downtown where we would celebrate by dancing the night away. I don't think God really approved of this part of the night, as the rain started to pour like crazy.

We arrived at the Spanish night club, rushed in from the rain and spent the night doing the samba and the merengue. I must admit it was a great way to end off the night, however the night was nowhere close to being finished, for me and Renata at least. After the club we had arranged for the limo to take us home so we could grab our packed suitcases and fly out to the Dominican Republic. Let the honeymoon begin.

We spent seven days in the Dominican enjoying the sun, the beach, the food and adapting to the newly married life. On the first night we went out to the beach late at night when no one was there. The sky was full of stars and the sound of the ocean echoed beautifully. We talked about how wonderful our wedding was, and how fast it went. We reminisced on every moment and how grateful we were for our true family and friends.

Punta Cana, where we stayed, was absolutely beautiful. The weather was perfect for us all seven days that we were there. The beach was crystal clear and the people at the hotel were fantastic hosts. They told us all about life in the Dominican, and we learned so much about their culture and how they lived. I even learned a few Spanish words! Renata and I also entertained a few conversations about the plans for our life when we got

HOW?

back, but nothing concrete, after all it was a honeymoon not a board meeting. The greatest part for me without a doubt was the food! Endless, unlimited food, available at anytime of the day. I was truly in paradise. Eggs and sausages for breakfast, fresh fish for lunch, and a fancy Italian dinner to close off the night. If we got hungry in the middle of the night, we would just walk over to one of the restaurants and pick up some wings and fries. It was truly an unforgettable time for us as a newly married couple. But just like our wedding, the week had flown by. We packed our bags and got ready to start heading back home to Canada and back to work. Adios, Punta Cana!

SACRIFICE

After what felt like a fairytale, it was time for Renata and I to get the ball rolling on real life and get myself refocused on opening my own franchise. As soon as I got home, I put the pedal to the metal and dove right into work. I was on a new mission, and that was to learn everything I needed to know in order to accelerate my franchisee training. As time went on, I continued my training to become a contributing part of the positive company culture, sales growth and marketing efforts. The environment was always so positive and fast paced that it created the perfect atmosphere for creative ideas and improvements. Werner did a great job at always keeping the team motivated and frequently planned exciting incentives for the managers. About a month after we had returned from our honeymoon, Werner announced a sales contest between the managers where we were given two months to see which manager could raise the most amount of sales by conducting some kind of extra service that wasn't presently offered. The winner would receive a paid vacation to Las Vegas. Now, this is when Pizza gets very interesting. My partner Steve and I knocked our brains together and came up with some innovative ways of

HOW?

creating new customers and pushing for more sales. For two months, we worked our butts off, coming up with coupon ideas, creating a Facebook page for the store and giving the best customer service we could. After all, a free trip to Vegas? This isn't something that just happens everyday. After what seemed like forever, the big day finally arrived. Werner was ready to announce the winners! Steve and I were exhausted, but very confident that we had done our best.

When the announcement was complete, sure enough our efforts had paid off! Steve and I had won the trip to Vegas! We had successfully managed to increase our store's sales enough to enjoy a free trip to the infamous Sin City. What made it even more special is that I got to bring a guest along with me, so Renata packed her bags and we, alongside Steve and his guest, Werner and his wife and the entire senior management team headed for the airport. It was a wonderful trip, filled with delicious foods, cool hotels, flashy casinos and many amazing experiences that I'd love to share with you, but whatever happens in Vegas stays in Vegas, sorry.

Being the manager of a pizza shop was great, but being a pizza delivery boy was even better! It was required of me to work at least one pizza delivery shift per week to make sure I knew my surrounding area and how to work it effectively. This was always my highlight of the week. I loved meeting new people, and seeing the excited, hungry faces satisfied when the pizza guy arrived. I felt like an everyday hero, with my car full of pizzas. At times I was thrown into some of the most awkward positions, whether it be an all girls sleepover and having to turn down the invitation to join their soiree, or walking into a house packed with sweaty, drunk football fanatics who looked like they were going to eat me and the pizza at the same time. It was crazy, but it was good fun and to top it all off, the tips were an added bonus. The dream was in motion, I loved my job, I loved the people I worked for and the people I worked with and my very own pizza shop was in the horizon. As a franchisee in training for Yummy's Pizza, I had finally got to a point in my life where I felt settled. I learned some real valuable skills and I was bringing in the dough, literally. So what do you think? How about I end the book here and just call it a day? It's amazing how many times we would've ended our own stories if it were left up to us but the truth is, life is the real author of our stories and it's very capable of changing, rearranging or adding chapters in times when we least expect it. My story was far from over, and even Yummy's Pizza (the dream job) would soon become another chapter written, enjoyed and transformed into a memory.

It was when we got back from Las Vegas that Renata and I actually settled into life. Everything thus far had been a dream, from me deciding at the hospital that I wanted to get married, being engaged, and travelling to the Dominican and the U.S. However, the time had come for us to find our routine. Renata got a job at a photo studio at the mall right across the street from where we lived, while I was now full fledged in the last stages of my training. It was the two of us against the world. The next few months could easily be categorized as the building stages. The building stages in anyone's life is a time of many new beginnings and many first experiences. I got a taste of paying for water and hydro, I got a taste of having to cook everyday, furnish our home, manage the bills, make sure the car payment and insurance are in the bank and all that other exciting grown up stuff. This is what most people would call real life. As you get older, work becomes more serious and you take on new responsibilities.

We had rented out a beautiful brand new condo. It was on the twenty-seventh floor, of a sparkling glamorous building, full of cool amenities like a swimming pool and a virtual golf room. When you walked into the lobby, the friendly concierge and the cascading waterfall wall always greeted you. It was a beautiful rippled; stonewall, with a

HOW?

light stream of water gently running down it. It was the most beautiful building I had ever been in, and an exciting place to come home to everyday. Responsible adult life sure was different, but it was pretty cool.

As responsibility set in, work life became very real, and very time consuming. Having to pay bills began to take its toll as we had to gather all the money that we were so used to saving and start putting it towards rent, and hydro, and credit cards and old debts. Thankfully we always had enough to meet all of our needs, but we had to put in the hard work. With the intense workload, our time together as a newly married couple started to dwindle away.

Saturday mornings became our favourite time. I used to always look forward to it because it was the only day of the week when my wife and I were both off from work. Usually our schedules were perfectly fashioned in a way that ensured we'd never see each other. Monday morning, Renata started her shift at 9:00 a.m. Since we lived right across the street from the mall, there was no need for her to drive to work or for me to drive her because it was literally a five-minute walk. She woke up, got ready, made breakfast, kissed me on my forehead (as my cheek was a little bit too close to my drool marks) and then she was gone. By the time noon rolled around I would wake up, get ready, make breakfast and then relax on the couch until about 4:00 p.m. when I would then start heading out to get to begin my evening shift at 5:00 p.m. Renata would finish work at 5:00 p.m. and make her way home to an empty condo suite with a love note on the kitchen table expressing how much I missed her. I assume she probably took a nice shower, called up her friends or her family and invited them over to the condo to play golf or go swimming. By the time 7:00 p.m. rolled around, I was covered in cornmeal and tomato sauce with pizzas coming out of the oven left, right and center. By 1:30 a.m. I usually would have already taken the last delivery order and began the infamous store cleaning, which would usually take a minimum of one hour to get the store back into shape for the next day. At 2:00AM I started to close all the tills and do all the money counting, and by 2:30AM I had counted the money four times over trying to find a valid reason for my confusion. By this point I was tired, confused and frustrated, as I had already received Renata's "Dan, I'm going to bed- sorry I can't wait up anymore" phone call.

The clock strikes 3:00 a.m. I finally finished up the end of day cash out. After my 20-minute drive home, I usually push the key in the door gently at around 3:30 a.m. I would enter a dark, quiet condo suite with a love note taped to a saran wrapped dinner that reads something like: "Hey Darling! I hope you had a wonderful day at work. I miss you and I love you and I hope you enjoy this dinner I made for you, Love Ren (heart xoxo)" Slowly, this became the story of my life.

Most people find themselves in this place; a routine that offers some level of comfort in hopes of a desired lifestyle, but no actual time for living. This very true observation started to become my sad reality. I was happily married and I had a very promising career, but the things I really enjoyed felt like they were being robbed from me. I felt that despite the amazing opportunity I was endowed with, there was nothing else to look forward to except one day moving out to the country side to build my pizza store, where I would work 100 hours a day. If I was hardly seeing my wife and family now, how would it be when I actually got my franchise? I knew that in the long run I'd be well off, and that sacrifices were necessary for success, but at what expense?

The plain old routine life I always feared as a teenager started happening to me and my wife and this really made me think. I guess it could easily be said of me that I'm just an ungrateful North American man who is never content with what he has. I mean after all, I was only 22 years old, having bounced back from almost losing my life into a

HOW?

beautiful marriage, driving a decent vehicle, living in a luxury condo in the heart of a beautiful city. I was healthy and maintaining a promising management role in a big pizza franchise, and basically everything that once seemed completely impossible for me was happening. So what in the world could I be complaining about? Does this mean I'm an awful person? I wasn't necessarily complaining about my job or anything, but I definitely knew that something was missing. After taking some deep thought into how I was feeling, I found the answer.

One of the greatest words I have ever discovered and one of the main contributing factors to our company's continual growth today is discomfort. Comfort in some way can be the killer of dreams and aspirations, because it somehow convinces you that you have arrived in a "safe place" and you should have enough common sense to remain there. The problem with that is, what if you're not happy there? What if you believe there is more to your journey? This is where the word discomfort comes in and challenges you to go further. Discomfort is one of the biggest influencers of change. It seems that regardless of the fortunate opportunities one may have in life, it is the discomfort that urges us to go further and reminds us that contentment never brings about change, and change is something that is much needed in our world today. Entrepreneurs understand this philosophy and discomfort is what drives them on a daily basis. It's a simple theory but if you really consider it, it actually makes a whole lot of sense. You never get a new bed until you're uncomfortable with your old one.

Imagine one day a super powerful hurricane came headed right for your house; you try to hide and take shelter but the size and strength of the boisterous windstorm makes it very clear that there is absolutely no escaping its path. With your arms curled around your head and your knees tightly tucked in to your chest, you shield yourself into a ball and close your eyes tight hoping for the best. The wrath of the winds immediately sweep you off of your feet and send you flying in every direction, something you had never planned for and had no idea where you would eventually end up. As you're tossed to and fro like tumbleweed on a windy day, all kinds of different particles and materials are stirred up in the windstorm with you and the speed and strength of the wind makes these particles very dangerous and possibly lethal if they hit you in the wrong place. You're cut, you're bleeding, you're bruised and in the same heartbeat you suddenly fall to the ground as the soft grass of a distant pasture cushions your fall. You slowly open your eyes as strong beams of sunlight burst inside causing you to squint. There's an amazing calm and quietness that surrounds you and you realize that you have just entered the eye of the storm. Although this might sound like a page ripped right out of the movie Twister, it's not. This metaphorical picture was my life up until this point, (please re-read if you must.) Scarred, battered, cut and tossed I now found myself in a peaceful place in my life. I was in the eye of the storm and it was beautiful. As a newly married man, I was very proud to be able to show my new wife that I had found stability for once in my job allowing me to put her mind at ease. When I ran into old friends I could now speak confidently of my management position at Yummy's Pizza and my short-term future goals of opening my own Yummy's Pizza franchise instead of saying "I'm just doing the music thing," or "just factory grinding." Renata and I moved into a beautiful luxury condo and every now and then we enjoyed the many amenities of our condo with friends when they would come over, nothing but good times and new adventures. Weather specialists have often said that a person on the ground walking in the eye of a hurricane could see blue skies in the day or stars at night if the eye is free of widespread clouds. The skies sure looked blue to me and the stars were illuminated in the most magical way. I thought I had discovered the pathway to success.

HOW?

I always grew up hearing quotes and statements about success like, "no sacrifice, no reward," or "sweat plus sacrifice equals success" and for the most part I get it, you had to work hard to be successful. But really what is sacrifice? What does it mean? I would soon come to realize that sacrifice can be likened to a person that lives in the eye of a hurricane, has the option of remaining there forever and willingly chooses to run right back into the hurricane just to see if they'll make it out alive. That is sacrifice and that is what it takes to be an entrepreneur. I know this because I did it, in the midst of a peaceful calm and quietness, I decided to run back into the boisterous winds risking everything my wife and I had attained just to see if maybe there was something worth discovering on the other side of the storm... if we made it out.

The epiphany happened one early morning when Chad accompanied me on a drive out where I was expected to visit some of the nearby schools in hopes of winning their business for the upcoming pizza day lunches. A new school year has just begun. These school contracts made up a significant portion of our sales as the schools would sometimes order hundreds of pizzas to facilitate the demand set by the students. The quality of our pizza was undeniable, so really and truly, winning the contracts was simply based on who was sent to talk to these schools, what was said, the timing and the ensured guarantee that the pizza day lunches would run smoothly every week. Chad and I pulled up in front of one of the local schools that Werner had mentioned we had been trying to get in contact with and I took the blank contract, motioned to Chad to wait for me and I walked into the school. After I had found the main office and had properly explained my reason for being there, they took the contract had a look over it, signed it and gave it back. And just like that we had just added a new school, a new opportunity and a new income stream to our shop in only a matter of ten minutes. As I took hold of the signed contract and headed towards

the school exit I remember thinking to myself,
"It's that simple?" "really?" Then what in the world is stopping me from presenting a contract to someone to sign for some kind of product or service that I offered? I know I'm not afraid to introduce myself to people or to conduct a small presentation, so why have I never entertained the thought of doing exactly what I'm doing at this moment for myself? I realized that if I could do this for myself then maybe it would even get to the point where I could hire someone like myself to go out and win client contracts and eventually get my time back with my wife and my family. An excited bubbly feeling of endless possibilities began to erupt inside of me as I approached my car outside of the school. "Ouch!"
The entrepreneurial bug had just bitten me and the effects were spreading throughout my body very fast.

 I no longer wanted to be the person that only follows the rules. I wanted to experience what it was like to make the rules. I no longer wanted my team and employees to trust me based on my progress. Instead I wanted to hire and build my own team who will trust me because of a proven process that I teach to them. I no longer wanted to spend my day running around to persuade people as to why they should choose the company I work for. I'd rather spend my entire life running around persuading people to believe in a company that I built. My eyes lit up like a child that just received their favourite toy at Christmas, and I couldn't wait to open this new gift. I ran to the car as I really wanted to tell Chad all about this new light bulb that just flicked on in my head and explain to him my new perspective about life, business and careers. I headed towards the car as if I was attempting to run right back into the wall of the hurricane ready to sacrifice everything and see where this gust of wind might take me next. Sure enough that's exactly what was about to happen.

 As I entered into the car, Chad immediately said, "Ok what happened? Why do you have that weird look on your

HOW?

face?"

I smiled really big.

I began blurting out all my thoughts and explaining how we could be doing so much more with our lives and how we have so much more potential than we have ever realized. He took a deep breath as if to say, "here we go again."

And that was it. From that moment on I knew that I was going to do what ever it took to start my own business and be my own boss.

The rest of that week was one of the hardest weeks for me in terms of future planning. It's one thing to get excited about the thought of starting your own business, but right after that thought really sets in, you naturally begin to see all the roadblocks, walls and reasons why it might not work based on your current situation or financial situation. The dream you so passionately embraced now sits in the balance of dream versus reality. I felt so confused because inside I believed that starting my own business would be the best decision for my wife and I, but all that I would be forced to sacrifice to even try something like this could be detrimental to our future which we are just in the process of building. Dang! I guess it's not at easy as I thought.

I invited Jon and Chad over for a night of good conversation that we would have every now and then, when our schedules would permit it. I needed some time to brainstorm with my two closest friends to figure out exactly where my head was at with my newfound idea. I told them that I wanted to start my own business, and that I wanted it to be something that was focused on the overall customer experience. I wanted to exceed people's expectations and make them feel special. After all I had been through, this was all that really mattered to me. They agreed that the motive was a good one.

As we were talking, Chad asked, "so what kind of business do you want to start? Is it a restaurant, or a clothing store or a pizza shop? Where are you actually going to apply this great service?"

I couldn't answer his question yet. All I knew was that I wanted to give excellent customer service, but the uncertainty of what I was going to make or sell ended up in a heated debate. They both thought I was nuts for saying that I wanted to start a business that offered great service but I didn't have a product or service.

"So, you're telling me that you are actually going to leave Yummy's, and you don't even know what you're really going to do? That doesn't make any sense!"

To a certain degree they were right. I didn't have plans to just walk out of my job. But I believed that although my plan wasn't crystal clear, I did have a plan. Instead of figuring out what I was going to do, I focused on what I had promised myself I would do. Now it was simply a matter of deciding where to apply this promise.

(Inner thought says)

"Seriously Daniel? You actually land a good, secure job considering the limited amount of credentials and educational certification that you have, you just got married, and now you want to leave it? Daniel, don't be dumb. If you give this up now, you are going to fail everyone that believed in you whether it be your wife, your parents, Werner and the management team who believed I would be next up in line to open my own Yummy's Pizza shop. You'll fail the employees you manage, as you will have cut your relationship right at a point where they were beginning to trust you. Most of all, you will fail yourself because you will have to take responsibility for all these people you have let down."

This is usually the part when that person running toward the hurricane wall feels the whiplash of the powerful wind touch their skin and they turn back and start running toward the eye of the hurricane once again, in desperate search of that peace, calm and quietness. Many aspiring entrepreneurs find themselves here, at the cliff of an idea looking out at the city of possibility with the depth of risk separating the two. What do you do? Although I can't answer that question for anybody but myself, I can say that entrepreneurs jump. Many like to paint a picture of entrepreneurs as people who don't calculate the risks of their decisions before they make them and that is not far from the truth. An entrepreneur is someone who weighs their options, calculates the risks and even when it seems like it might be too risky, they still do it. I'm glad I understood this even when I never understood this. Deciding to sacrifice, is to willingly surrender something or someone that belongs to you, while being fully aware of the possibility of never getting it or them back again. I also learned this lesson from The Holy Bible in the example of God sending his only son Jesus Christ to die for people that never knew him, never believed in him or even cared about what he was doing. It seems that I could never expire the lessons taught in the Bible as they could so easily be applied to my life and every time I read it I learned something new. Not everyone is willing to give up what they have to potentially attain what they want or need, but whether one is willing or not, sacrifice is inevitable. You either give up what you have to get what you want, or you give up what you want to keep what you have. It all boils down to making that choice. I was at a place in my life where I was willing to give up everything I had to explore the possibility of getting everything I ever wanted, and lucky enough it worked.

So I decided, I would gradually find a way to start building a new dream, one that was tailored for me, for my wife, my family and for the things that I valued the most in this life; leaving a positive impact on people's lives, serving others and taking crazy ideas and turning them into realities. Now, where to start?

THE APPLE TREE

The most frequently asked question that people often ask me is, "What made you start a tea business? Why tea? What was that Aha moment?"
You see it all started one day as I was comfortably sitting under a beautiful tree, when all of a sudden this apple fell... O wait, that was Sir Isaac Newton!

Truth be told, there was no single event that took place that I can say, this is what made me start a tea company. It was a combination of different things, all of which played an important role in bringing about T By Daniel. When I juggled the idea of starting my own business I literally had to conduct a process of elimination, I knew what I was really good at and I also knew what I was terrible at. Many things I thought of required certification or an enhanced level of skill that frankly I just didn't have. Obviously there are many other paths in life that one can take that wouldn't require intense training, or years of schooling and experience, it was just a matter of time before I found one that suited me. I decided to refocus my attention on the things that were important to me at that present time in my life. The stabbing incident was obviously one of the biggest and most recent incidents in my life that caused a major shift in my thinking. I wanted to do something with my life that gave me a sense

HOW?

of purpose, something that allowed me the opportunity to impact people's lives every single day. I knew now that I didn't want to sit behind a computer all day writing computer codes and html hyperlinks in hopes of creating the next big tech startup. I wanted to be around people, and I wanted to interact with humans not machines. I wanted to talk face to face with people and hear about their lives and their families and all the wonderful things that make their journey through life so unique.

I was so convinced about my decision to take the leap into entrepreneurship, that I decided to make all the necessary changes in my life to facilitate this next jump. First I talked to my Renata and explained to her that I was no longer excited about my position at Yummy's and that I wanted to do something unique, rewarding and impactful with my life. Renata has always believed in me and always rooted for me in whatever I decided to do in life and that's what I loved about her. I guess she believed that if I was able to find a way to pay for our Boston Pizza tab, then I could probably figure out life and all its complexities. I told Renata that I was going to talk to Werner about my position at Yummy's Pizza and explain to him and the team that I no longer wanted to work towards establishing a pizza franchise. Basically I wanted to quit, but I also didn't want to just leave Werner and my Yummy's Pizza team high and dry.

At first I was really excited! But then the thought of leaving Yummy's actually began to haunt me. Although I felt ready to start my own voyage and start building my own dreams, I felt as if I was letting Werner down and ruining his dream. I battled with that thought for months before ever mentioning to Werner that I wanted to start my own business. I just thought that he would feel so let down, because I had chosen to be apart of this pizza franchise and I committed myself to the plan. Werner Sr. and Werner Jr. had invested so much time and money in me, hoping that I would be one of their next franchise partners. So how in the world do I tell them, "thanks for all your time, for the paid trip to Vegas and 7 star hotel adventures, free pizzas and great salary but I actually don't want to open up a pizza store anymore." Even though this was not the way I viewed their generosity and my job perks, I just couldn't imagine how they could take it any other way. I'm not certain about its origin, but there is a famous saying that goes "You'll either become an entrepreneur, or you'll end up working for one." The truth of that statement alone helped to fortify my thoughts to start my own business.

I decided to go and talk to my most trusted advisors, my mom and dad. I don't know what it is about my parents, but for some reason every time I talk to them about anything, I always leave that conversation with a lot more clarity and a better game plan. They agreed that I shouldn't continue to work towards something if I wasn't 100% passionate about it and they also pointed out the valuable tip about living as oppose to existing. Some people are living life, enjoying what they do, enjoying their families, they are present in whatever comes their way. Then there are people who are just existing. These kinds of people are going through the motions of life, but they are not really present, mainly because they are not happy with their lives and thus do not experience fulfillment.

As I touched on earlier, the intense level of responsibility I had as the general manager of Yummy's Pizza usually resulted in me working six days a week and "on call " on the seventh day. I would clock in way more than fourty hours a week, and because I struggled so badly with completing the end of day store cash out, I would usually end up coming home as late as 4:00 a.m. in the morning trying to find out why the store was short five hundred dollars. It was always something really stupid that I just overlooked or counted wrong. The worst feeling of my life was having to call Werner at 3:00 a.m. in the morning, waking him out of his sleep just for him to ask,

HOW?

"Dan, did you count all the money in the safe as well?"
"... Uhh. Oops." Sure enough, there was the missing five hundred dollars. The point is, my parents felt that it was important for me to actually enjoy my quality of life, even if that meant downscaling the luxuries that we were enjoying. After all, what's the point in living in a luxury condo with fabulous amenities that you never use? How will you build a strong marriage if you never get to spend time with your wife? They stressed the importance of these things and it really helped me gain a better perspective about my life and the decision I was about to make. I knew that starting my own business would be harder than being the manager of someone else's, but the benefit that I saw was that I would get to build at my own pace, and I would get to build it with my family, instead of always trying to fit them into my schedule. My parents concluded by advising that I keep my job until I knew exactly what I wanted to do and as they always used to say when I was younger, "just sit down, relax and have a cup of tea. Don't let life stress you out."

Now in order for me to scale down my lifestyle I knew there would be some sacrifices. We were paying far too much in rent, to possibly be able to save anything to get our business started. Since we already owed money to credit cards and loans, the thought of taking out a business loan was not an attractive one. The first thing that had to go was our beautiful condo lifestyle. Unfortunately, it just didn't fit the profile for an aspiring entrepreneur with no capital. My parents knew that in order for this to be possible, we were going to need a whole lot of help. Being the caring parents that they are, they extended an invitation to my wife and I for us to leave the condo lifestyle and move back home. WHAT! ARE YOU SERIOUS? This was the greatest invitation I had ever received in my life! Moving back home would alleviate so much financial pressure off of our marriage and it would definitely make it a lot easier to focus on starting my business. Now they didn't promise us a free ride, and I would never accept to take one, but I knew things would feel much lighter and having my parents and advisors within arms reach would be key in moving our lives forward.

Now this was no "flip of the wand" decision. I still had to make sure my wife was on board with the decision to leave a luxury condo, privacy, and a five minute walk to work and trade it all in for a forty-five minute bus ride to work, a full house, and one humble sized bedroom. Basically we would be starting from scratch.

When I came home that night with the news from my parents, I knew both my wife and I were faced with a big decision. Although Renata did look relieved, she knew that this was a huge compromise of what she was used to. Life was not about to get easier, and there would be many more challenges we would have to overcome. But at least this way, we could overcome them together, instead of overcoming everything on our own. Fortunately, my wife understood that the pros outweighed the cons. So we broke our lease, packed a few bags and we were back home to my old bedroom.

#DansBizTip:

My dad once told me, "never despise the days of humble beginnings."

Pride can be a very dangerous thing. Sometimes our pride is so strong that it weakens our ability to make good decisions. Over the years, I've met so many people who have expressed to me that they too dream of starting their own business and being their own boss but they're not willing to leave their good jobs to go knocking on doors, cold calling people or trying to get people to sample their products as they walk by at a trade show. The first thing I think to myself is, well, how good is your current job if you're always dreaming of leaving it? Second, I think,

HOW?

really? Why can't you knock on someone's door or offer them a sample to try? What is the worst that could happen? Chances are it's not because you can't do it. It's because you are afraid that you'll hear the word "no", or you'll hear, "we're not interested." But what if the person says yes? What if you tried something and people actually liked it? The biggest reason why we're afraid to hear the word "no!" is because it takes a shot at our pride. We subconsciously feel that the whole world should shout "YES!" to us all the time, because we're so cute, we're so right, and we're so smart. For us to expect a certain answer from someone, because of the way we feel about ourselves, is both selfish and silly at the same time. Allow people to exercise their will to choose instead of getting offended when they say no to you. The moment you detach yourself from the embarrassment, offense, nervousness and disappointment of hearing the word "no!" you automatically start to focus your attention on celebrating and making the best out of the "yes's."

Pride doesn't allow you to think this way. I apply this to my life and teach it to my employees and we always rock out at tradeshows because of it. Hundreds, sometimes thousands of people walk by our booth at tradeshows and we try to talk to everyone and offer them samples or an opportunity to come and learn about what we're selling. Some people say 'no' politely and some people even get offended that we asked and give us a mean grumpy face. We either focus on the next person or sometimes use that 'no' as an opportunity to try and turn that person into a 'yes!' Regardless if we succeed or not, we definitely celebrate our effort of asking. After all, it's only out of asking that you will ever hear a "yes!"

Ok, two down and one more to go. My wife was on board with me, my parents are on board, and now I just needed to break the news to Werner. I thought long and hard about what I would say to him and then I realized that maybe I should really solidify exactly what kind of business I was going to start before I actually quit my job or else that would sound really stupid. "Hey Werner, I just wanted to let you know that I'm quitting my job to think about what kind of business I should, uhh, start." Yeah, not a good idea. Still motivated, I decided to continue trying to figure out what I was going to do first before I made any sudden changes.

One night, Renata decided to go out for a bite to eat with one of her good friends and that meant I had the home all to myself. I remember pulling out my laptop and sitting at the kitchen table surfing the net looking for some form of inspiration or a creative business idea. I searched and searched and found nothing. When you're Googling, it usually takes you a little while to actually find the best way of typing in your desired search phrase in a way that will actually bring back good results. Finally, I decided to Google "List of possible businesses to start." Hundreds of results immediately popped up but my eyes were drawn to a link that said "The Easiest Businesses To Start From A-Z." It was incredible! I actually found a list of various types of creative business ideas for me to consider, some of which required little to no experience. This was like a treasure chest of possibilities for me to explore. Let's begin. I went through the entire list, from A to Z and was fascinated at how many possible business ideas there were out there. There were lots of cool concepts, but nothing that really sparked the flame. One business idea came really close when I found 'Hallmark card maker.' I read it and thought to myself, hey that's different; imagine spending my entire day sitting down and writing poems and warm fuzzy greetings for Hallmark cards… suddenly, making pizzas for the rest of my life didn't look so bad. I still couldn't find anything, therefore I continued to toss pizzas, sprinkle cheese and wait for some shiny red apple to fall out of a tree and hit me on my head.

Alas! It was Saturday. Finally Renata and I could spend some quality time together. One Saturday, we

HOW?

decided to head to our local mall just to walk around, window-shop and grab a bite to eat. As we were casually strolling through the newly updated mall, a bright teal looking sign stood out in my peripheral vision and when I took a closer look, the store name read DAVIDSTEA. Renata and I had the whole morning to spend, and being that we were in absolutely no rush to leave the mall, we decided to walk by and have a look at this new shop. First I was drawn in by the unique colour scheme of this shop, which was so different than every other store in the mall. Second, I wondered what DAVIDSTEA actually meant, as I was certain that the store couldn't be referring to tea as in the tea that you drink. Or could it? There's no way a tea shop could look so cool, so modern and so stylish. I've been drinking tea all my life as a child and I only know tea to be chamomile, peppermint or lemon tea; boring and something you only drink when you're sick.

"Hey guys! How's it going today? Would you like to try out our tea sample of the day?"

An extremely happy freckle-faced ginger decided to help settle our curiosity by greeting us and offering us a sample of their tea of the day. I replied by asking if she meant tea as in like peppermint and chamomile. She confirmed that we were talking about the same thing and that's when I started to become very intrigued. We headed into the brightly illuminated DAVIDSTEA shop and the rest was history. Renata and I sampled teas, smelled teas, explored teas, asked questions about teas and learned so many new things about a beverage, which to me had previously seemed completely outdated and snobby. For the first time in my life, I actually thought tea was kind of cool. That same day, I bought a sample kit of teas to bring home and steep. "Steep" was a new terminology in my world that I would soon become very familiar with. The aromas of the teas I bought followed me all through the mall and every couple of minutes I would reach into my teal, kraft DAVIDSTEA shopping bag and reach for one of them and pop it open just to take another whiff. It made me so happy and I was super excited to see how the smell of these teas would translate into my mug at home. Sure enough, I got home and rushed to turn on my kettle to try out my new aromatic treasures. I waited patiently for the water to boil and then I followed the brewing instructions on the package, remembering to let the boiling water cool down first before pouring it over the loose tealeaves, as my friendly ginger-haired tea fairy cautioned me. Doing so would burn the leaves giving me a bitter and harsh tasting tea. I poured, it steeped, I sipped and I fell in love all over again. If Renata were a tangible product, she would be tea. OK maybe that is a bit of a stretch but I'm sure you understand that I'm trying to say that I became instantly infatuated with loose leaf tea and this was the beginning of my tea journey. That night I went on to try out all of the other tea blends that I had purchased from DAVIDSTEA and I remember being blown away that their tea descriptions and tea names were so accurate in how the tea tasted. It's almost like the name of the tea played a major role in the experience, at least it did for me personally. I was so impressed with this new company and I had to know more about it. Is there really a David in DAVIDSTEA? Who is he and why and how did he discover this awesome, hidden world of tea? When did this company start? As all these questions popped into my head, I began researching the company.

As I Googled the night away sipping my delicious loose-leaf teas, I began to unfold a much bigger picture than just DAVIDSTEA. In fact, it turned out that specialty teashops were popping up everywhere! There was a very close competitor of DAVIDSTEA called Teaopia, which was founded right in my city at the time, Mississauga! Huh? Something special was brewing and I wanted to find out what it was. From that day forward, I became so obsessed with visiting every teashop in the GTA to discover what kinds of teas and herbal infusions were out

HOW?

there. With my nose leading the way I visited every teashop I could find buying little amounts of tea to see which flavours, types and aromas would become my favourites. After weeks of finding my new love for tea, I easily gave up on sugary juices, pops and wine and replaced them with loose-leaf tea. I started doing some online research about the health benefits of tea because I figured it's got to be good for something, and my findings were life changing! Certain teas focused on stress relief as other teas help aid in weight loss. As a matter of fact, some teas even had cosmetic benefits like helping to enhance blonde streaks in your hair or teas that could be used as a face mask to give your skin a natural glow. All of my findings were amazing and I wanted to share this information with everyone. I remember one afternoon I was lucky enough to get a day off, so I headed downtown Toronto to a local teashop in hopes of meeting a lady who was praised on several online review sites for her knowledge about tea, friendly service and authentic tea selection. Her shop was called House Of Tea. Her store was located close to the more affluent areas of Toronto. It was a small shop, quaint with a unique outdoor décor. As I opened the green shop door and peeked my head into the simple traditional teashop, a small, Sri Lankan lady named Marisha, who was the shop owner that I had hoped to meet, immediately greeted me. I entered the shop with curious yet amazed eyes, as I wanted to see what everyone was raving about online concerning this teashop. The shop was covered in a worn out wooden floor and what looked like two-hundred and fifty tins of different teas stocked on an endless shelving unit fastened to the wall. Before engaging in a conversation with Marisha, I motioned to her that I was going to take a second to look around the shop. I grazed my hands against the iron teapots; I examined the strainers and the teacups and saucers and made my way back to the front counter where I began talking to Marisha. I explained to her that I was a novice in tea and was hoping to gain a deeper knowledge about the delicious leaf, its benefits, its many flavours and I even threw in a few questions about selling tea as a business.

My encounter with Marisha was nothing short of amazing. She was kind and very knowledgeable due to her own personal experiences in working on an actual tea plantation in Sri Lanka, and running a tea business. She pulled down so many different canisters of teas and taught me all about each one. She talked to me about the right way to brew them, the amount to use, the quality and freshness, the different flushes, (which meant a time in which the leaves were harvested.) After, a very informative conversation, I purchased a few teas, and Marisha insisted that I take a few free samples home of some of her most popular oolongs, pu-erhs, and herbal tisanes. I felt like a kid who went trick-or-treating for the first time, no costume necessary. I thanked Marisha and exited the store feeling super inspired about drinking these authentic teas. I felt so honoured to have spent the last hour with a woman who in my eyes was like a tea guru! When I got home that evening, I quickly showed Renata all my new tea findings. I pulled out all of my new teas and began trying to re-teach my wife all the new information I had just learned. She became very intrigued with the knowledge I shared with her, but she was also annoyed that I was subtly becoming a tea hoarder. At work, I became known as Mr. Tea or The Tea Guy because everyday I was at the shop brewing these different teas on my break, sharing the smell of the beautiful aromas with my fellow co-workers. My family knew me as the tea guy, my wife knew me as the tea guy, and my friends started referring to me as the tea guy. *KAPLUNK!* I think that's the sound of an apple falling.

T

That was it. My mind was made up and I decided to choose the life of risk, challenges and discomfort as far as my career was concerned. I knew that my decision to start my own business would not be an easy one, I knew I would probably have to work harder than I've ever worked and make less money than I've ever made, but I was ready and I was willing.

On January 1, 2011, while most of my old friends were probably popping bottles of champagne in downtown Toronto celebrating the New Year, I had just come back from an amazing church service. I welcomed the New Year in with a prayer of thanksgiving and went home with my wife in a mind state of deep reflection. By no means am I implying that I was better than my friends because I went to church on New Year's, but I think it's important to draw the contrast between what I would probably be doing to what I was actually doing at this point in my life. This was by far the most sober New Year's celebration I had ever experienced in a long time and I really enjoyed it.

There's a famous saying that states, " January 1st millions of goals are made, February 1st millions of goals are broken." My intention was to prove to myself that this statement wasn't true.

I had made the biggest step in my entrepreneurial venture. I now knew that the product that I was going to sell was tea. I had grown to love everything about tea, I enjoyed drinking it and smelling it and I figured, if done properly, tea would be the perfect tool for bringing people together, as it so naturally does. First things first, I knew I had to learn every possible thing about tea and business before I could start a real tea business. I had to become as confident as Marisha from the House Of Tea shop was if I was going to stand a chance at starting a successful venture. I took a casual trip to the dollar store, as I figured I would need to have a notebook to write down my ideas, my observations, my goals and create a thorough to-do list to keep track of my progress. This is a very basic step when starting out that pretty much shows you from the start that you are actually serious about what you're planning to do. I still promote this first step today when offering tips to aspiring entrepreneurs, as I find this dollar store voyage to be a very effective way of filtering out the driven people from the procrastinators. I purchased a shiny, psychedelic green notebook, a pen and a calculator and began my journey. Step two: The library. I knew that I didn't have extra money to invest in a full-fledged business education. I didn't even have enough savings at that point to enroll in a tea focused course. Knowing that I still needed to educate myself, I figured I would go to the one place that always offered free and valuable information. I went to my local library every single day, before or after work, to study books, videos, magazines and articles about tea. My desire to learn about this plant known as tea had me thumbing through hundreds of different books in the library, until one day I discovered a few books about tea by an author named Jane Pettigrew. I had no idea who she was, but I found her books to be very interesting and easy to understand. I signed out a few of her books and started

HOW?

burying my face in every page. I learned so much about the Camellia Sinensis plant, which is the actual Latin name of the tealeaf. When I wasn't studying books about tea in the library, I was at home experimenting with all types of different teas, herbs and steeping times, while recording all my observations in my newly created tea log. I paid special attention to three factors of every tea I would taste: the flavour, the aroma and the tea colour. These three components were vital in determining whether a tea was brewed correctly or even just to decide whether I liked a tea or not and maybe planned to make it a part of my collection when I launched my business. I eventually became so good at evaluating these three characteristics of a tea that in most cases, even if blindfolded, I could tell which tea I was drinking. I was really starting to carve out my niche. My focus had been shifted completely and all I could think about everyday was new ideas and creative ways of building this tea adventure into some kind of business.

You may be wondering at this point, how did I ever end up telling Werner that I was transitioning out of the pizza dream? Unfortunately, I have a precise step-by-step memory of how it all played out. All I know is that I mustered up the courage and did it. After explaining to Werner my decision to leave Yummy's, I felt as if the conversation kind of just floated in mid air for a day or two, because there wasn't much of a reaction, neither good nor bad. After a couple days of making my resignation known to Werner and his dad, I had a meeting with them, and they explained to me that they didn't want me to quit my job. They knew that I had a new goal but they wanted to try and accommodate it. They were willing to void me of pretty much all my manager duties and instead, offer me a new role in the company as a Customer Relations Coordinator.

Huh? Am I hearing this correctly?

Yes, they were actually willing to create a position for me

within the company just so I wouldn't leave. Now this was pretty awesome. I immediately became interested in hearing more about this new position and what it would entail, because I figured without the massive responsibility of being a manager, I would be able to spend more time working on my tea business and still have some form of income. Talk about a win-win situation!

Over the next couple of days, Werner explained to me that my new position, in a nutshell, was to go out to companies and basically try and win over their business. It was something that I had done before, especially going to schools trying to get pizza contracts, only now I would be expanding into corporate offices. This seemed unreal. It was almost like they were giving me a taste of running my own business in preparation for running my own business. There was only one stipulation to obtaining this dream job. I would be fully responsible for training my replacement first. Hmm… Let me think about that one for a sec… Umm, YES PLEASE!

They say in life you can't always have your cake and eat it too. I'm actually not quite sure how that relates to anything, but it felt right to add that in there. I thought to myself, this is a great opportunity for me to transition in a wise way without leaving the team stranded without a manager. I accepted to stay and to train my replacement before demoting myself to my new position.

Interviewees started rolling in, and it wasn't until Werner met John, who would become my replacement, that he was ready to hire and get him trained. As months passed, I wasted no time training our newest hire John. He was a cool guy and a quick learner so it made my job a lot easier. Within no time, John was running shifts and I was officially demoted. The demotion came with its pros and definitely with its cons. By alleviating myself of my former managerial duties, I was now able to dedicate a numerous amount of hours towards building my tea business, but on the other hand I was only getting paid for the amount of hours I spent on the road visiting companies, which was not enough hours to make a living. I was faced with a critical choice at this point. Do I dedicate more hours to my new position so I can make a healthy pay cheque or do I grind this tea business thing out and try my absolute best to make it work quickly? With Renata still holding down her full time job, I decided to just stick with my small pay and get this tea business boiling. I visited almost every possible teashop I could find in the GTA and soaked up as much information as I could about tea and about running a tea business. I watched YouTube videos until my eyes were sore, and after months of studying and staying up late, I figured it was time to officially register my business. The most exciting part of registering a business has to be naming the business. When I was thinking about possible names for my company, I thought to myself it would be really cool if I had some kind of mystery or spontaneity to my business name or the company on a whole. I had always been a fan of Willy Wonka and the Chocolate Factory. There was something so magical about the Wonka World. I loved the many colours, and irony's, the hidden messages and the world of possibilities that Willy Wonka and his oompa-loompa's had created. I also loved the level of exclusivity that the factory maintained as only five children in the entire world had the opportunity to come inside and explore this sweet house of madness. It was this kind of mystery that inspired my business name.

On March 21, 2011, I officially registered my tea business under the name ' T.' Short, mysterious, and it left you wondering.

I loved it and I thought it was so simple yet so creative! When you look at the name it just looks like the letter 'T' but when you say it, you're actually unfolding the name and also what we sell, whether you know it or not. I envisioned one day having a store with tinted black mirrors so that you wouldn't be able see inside, and a simple, mysterious ' T ' on the front window. Think about how curious people would be to find out what's inside. The name gave you everything without giving you anything. I officially registered my business as a sole proprietor and I was beginning to feel like this might just work. Next up was the logo, the second most exciting part of starting a business. This part came surprisingly easy for me. I modeled my thinking after the McDonald's golden arches. That yellow bent-French fry 'M' once illuminated could be seen from a mile away. It was so bold and known and embedded in our minds from childhood, that there's no getting away it. Once you see that 'M', it's over; you are getting a Big Mac. I decided to apply this simple, yet memorable McDonald's magic technique to my logo creation. I thought maybe just a Times New Roman ' T ' could do the same thing. I started researching graphic designers, logo makers and artists and somehow found this lady who claimed that she was able to make logos. This was my original email to her: "Hi there,

First off, thanks for your interest in helping me design a logo. Here are the details. I want to design a logo for a Tea company; the company name is going to be ' T ' just plain and simple capital ' T '. I don't want any other words or letters (however don't hold back on your creativity). Ideally I would like to just have a big, bold, capital ' T ' with curly steam coming out of the top. Please feel free to add your touch, but try and just improve on my main idea."

After a few back and forth emails, we finally decided on a simple yet effective design of the letter ' T ' with three curly steams protruding out the top. At that point, it was the most perfect logo. Now along with the name and the logo, I also wanted to attach a catchy phrase or slogan to the company so that people would have something to remember me by. Here's what I came up with.

(Warning! They're super corny)

Slogan 1: Between me and you... I think it's time for change. (What the heck? Seriously Dan?)

Slogan 2: Tea, with a little style.

HOW?

Slogan 3: ' T ' is always in Be-T-ween.

All of these really sucked, and were anything but magical. But I stuck with "T is always in be-T-ween." Next step, I started researching all kinds of different tea suppliers all over the world to see how I could actually get my hands on some tea to sell. I found a supplier who seemed to be very knowledgeable and reputable in the tea industry and the great news was, their company was located right in Toronto. I sent out a few emails requesting some information about their teas and products and asked also if we could setup a meeting. The next day I received an email response confirming a time and place to meet and I was overjoyed. All this setting up meetings stuff was all new to me but I was always down for a new adventure. During my meeting with this amazing teashop owner, I learned so many new things. In fact, I couldn't even write down the bundle of information he shared with me about the industry, it was just too much. Before our meeting came to a close, he congratulated me on starting my business and slipped in a quick question asking me what the name of my tea company was. With a confident grin of creativity on my face, I replied, 'T.'
He looked at me with a confused kind of look and repeated after me saying,
' T? ' You mean just like the letter ' T '?
I thought to myself, by now he is probably so amazed with my level of creativity that he is blown away. He then replied and said,
"Isn't there a tea company in Vancouver that is called ' T? '
"Umm...I don't think so...?" I unconfidently replied.
"I'm pretty sure there is. Try looking online." He said.
I pulled out my computer, to quickly search for this so-called company… #FAIL! Major Fail. There was totally another tea company named ' T. '

Once again, life presented me with two options:

A) I continue operating as ' T ' because it is legal and available in my province. Technically, I could use the name anywhere in my province, but if I ever tried to use the name and send my products to someone in Vancouver, then I'm in super hot water! Or
B) Change the name.
"Mom...Dad...any advice?"

My dad who was a former driving school instructor for sixteen years use to have his own business and he was so well known throughout the city in the world of driving instructors. When I explained the name situation to him, his answer was very simple.
"Why don't you just add your name to it, Dan?"
T...By Daniel?

The way it sounded in my head was like a promotion for a luxury fragrance for men. Introducing the new 'T By Daniel.' It's like 'Victory By Giovanni' or 'Rouge By Chanel.' Needless to say, I liked it. It made me feel like I had my own fashion label or something. Now that my name was involved, I began to think to myself, why don't I market myself as the fashionable tea guy? I could use my face as a part of the brand and give it a more personal touch.

So without further adieu, I re-registered my business as T By Daniel. Oh and check this out. The former rapper in me helped me rearrange some words and I managed to come up with a new slogan...
"Today and Tomorrow Begin With T!"
KABOOM! Stella got her groove back! T By Daniel was officially registered as a sole proprietorship on May 24, 2011. How's that for a May 2- 4 weekend?

T "BYE-BYE" DANIEL

T By Daniel was now officially a registered business, however, I had not sold any teas as yet. Following the official name registration, I spent the next couple of months researching trademarks and copyrights, solidifying tea and accessory suppliers, setting prices, and thinking of creative ways of branding myself. The funny thing is, I had no real experience with any of these important details of starting a business. Sure I had some management skills from my experiences in the past, but starting your own business is a whole new ball game. Despite the negative outcome that emerged out of my aspiring music hustle, it would be wrong for me not to credit most of what I knew in business from that experience. As an aspiring music artist, it's very unlikely that you'll be making any money for quite some time and even if you do start making money, it's usually not everyday. It's no different in business and that's what the beginning stages of T By Daniel was like. Absolutely no income, yet everyday I would incur a lot of expenses in good faith that something would happen. Luckily, I was use to this kind of hustle already, so it grounded me. The hungry, passionate music artist understands that they must first discover a unique way of displaying their music or themselves to the general public in hopes that people might take interest in what they do, and who they are. With that in mind, I decided to start designing the tea packaging that I would be using. I treated it like an album cover. It had to tell some kind of story. I had absolutely no skills or experience in graphic design, but when you're working with a budget of -$0.00, you find ways to work it out. So I decided to open up Microsoft Word on my desktop and try my best to put something together. In regards to the design, I definitely knew what I didn't want. It may sound weird, but I didn't want T By Daniel to look like a traditional tea company. After all, it was the traditional, Victorian look of tea that kept me away from it for 22 years, and if I was planning on breaking people's stereotypes of this fine, modern beverage, it had to be different. I thought about my core reason for wanting to start a tea business and underneath my new love and passion for sharing quality loose leaf tea with everyone, the real reason was my desire to impact people's lives in a special way. That being said I found a free file of a silhouette of a man and a woman's face and placed each picture on the sides of the label template and then placed my T By Daniel logo in the middle. I pictured this design as my statement to the world that tea is that calming, tasty excuse for bringing people together. Every conversation, every celebration, even the hard times people experience; you'll always find a cup of tea in-between two people. Although the heart behind the concept was from a good genuine place, when I look back at it now, it was actually really poorly executed and one of the creepiest designs I had ever seen. I have been infamously known for marrying my ideas, so no matter what someone else has to say or how they feel about my idea, once I like it, I'm doing it. Renata did give her opinions about my creepy design, but I thought it was creative and abstract and I was really anxious to get my business rolling.

Finally all my tea labels were completed, my teas were

packaged in tins and I was ready for the world. I created a T By Daniel Facebook page, Twitter page, YouTube channel and an online ecommerce site (www.tbydaniel.com) and started trying to get the word out there about my products. One of the most effective methods I used to market my music was through videos. I made so many videos of different songs and live performances and sometimes-stupid videos that had nothing to do with my music, but I was able to create my own little fan base from these efforts. With that music strategy behind me, I figured I might as well do the same thing with my business and start trying to grow a new fan base. Every couple of days I uploaded another video of me trying a tea and talking about it, surveying random people on the streets about which teas they drink, which company they buy from and how much they're willing to spend. I uploaded contests to give away free tea to try and get some engagement online, I made Facebook posts and Twitter posts of the many health benefits of drinking tea, but nothing seemed to be working. I got no orders, no reposts, no new likes, and Chad was the only person participating in my contests. Hmph. This is nothing like music.

Usually in a startup business, one would simply consult their business plan to go over what the next steps or plan of action should be. If the business plan was completed properly and effectively, you could almost read it just the same way you would a navigational map when you're trying to get to a destination. There was only one problem. I never had a business plan. Of course, I read about the importance of writing a business plan during my Google researching and all the books I read during my library hibernation. In fact, it was always the suggested first step in starting a business because through it, you would be able to properly evaluate the risks and projected rewards. I guess sometimes excitement makes you overlook proper procedures, oops. I was making next to nothing, so it was hard to put any money together to invest in any marketing or advertising for T By Daniel. I did some research on different ways a startup business can actually grow and most of the results that turned up suggested things like small business bank loans, business credit cards, lines of credit, venture capital funding and government grants and financing. I thought back to that situation in my music journey where my group and I borrowed money from Charlie to help us fund a collaboration with that British rap duo. Yeah, I'd rather not stare down the barrel of a gun again. I decided I was not going to apply for any loans from anyone to grow this business; I was just going to have to figure something else out.

One day as I sat at my parents' kitchen table (which was technically my first makeshift office), brainstorming the next move with T By Daniel, I remember stumbling into a very interesting and inspiring article about bootstrapping businesses. The article's title was appealing enough that I could relax and dive into a good read, accompanied by my morning cream of Earl Grey. I began reading the article as it explained what the term 'bootstrapping' actually means. It referred to a grassroots mentality in business where the entrepreneur takes more of an organic hustle approach to growing their startup business. It mentioned things like asking for love funding from your trusted immediate family, a much more intimate and less intimidating form of a loan, where you are not expected to pay back right away as your family supports you in the trials and errors of growing a business. Love funding was more of an understanding your family had, rather than an investment on their end. Love funding was mostly given in very small amounts, which enabled the borrower to accomplish single highlighted tasks and pay back the loan as you grow and go along. The article also encouraged self-funding your own business by getting a part-time job or side gigs and using a percentage of that income to fund your startup. The article concluded by reiterating that a bootstrapping approach to business is not recommended for someone who is trying to grow their business fast or get rich quick. Growth could be very slow but it's a lot easier to grow your business while not having the weight of loans and debts on your back. Debt is probably the number one reason why most startup businesses fail within the first five years. Incurring huge debt before you have proven a concept is like killing your idea prematurely, as you're allowing others to take away from something that you haven't even finished making. Using a baker as an example, it's like the bank saying to you, "Let me take a bite out of each pie that you bake before you sell it." Yeah, how will you ever be able to sell a good pie if every pie has a big bite out of it? First, you should sell a few pies until you've proven that people will buy them, and once you have that proof you can now borrow money to make a lot more pies in so much that the bank can enjoy their own.

With this new knowledge of bootstrapping, I put on my best puppy face and asked my parents if they could lend me sixty dollars to get what I thought was a professional in studio video made, because I had a new idea! One day as I waited for my car to be serviced at the Honda dealership I used to work at, I was hanging out in the lounge and I went to make myself a coffee.
What?
A coffee...how dare you!
Well I had no alternative because they had the worst selection of tea bags...*Light bulb!*
AHA! I thought to myself, this is a multi-million dollar company and a world-renowned automobile brand and look at the poor quality of tea they offer their loyal customers! Everyone knows you can simply go to "I know a guy" mechanic shop and get the same servicing done to your car for a third of the price, so if you choose to get your car serviced at your home dealership you deserve to be treated as royalty. At least that's what I thought. After

this oil-changing moment, I decided that I was going to start offering my premium quality loose leaf teas to businesses instead of consumers only. Tada! I created the T By Daniel business-to- business package. This package was a solution to the poor quality of tea and limited tea options that businesses were offering to their clients and customers. For a little more than what they were already spending on low quality tea bags, I would come and create a new tea setup and menu for businesses to offer their customers a more elite tea experience, which I promised to the owners would provide a more exceptional experience for their much deserving customers. I wanted to roll this idea out with a bang because I was certain it would work. I needed the sixty dollars from my parents to pay for a one-hour session at a green screen studio. I would then take the promo video and pitch it to businesses such as car dealerships, hotels, spas, and basically anywhere that offered tea.

I was beside myself the day a hair salon actually emailed me back expressing their interest in sampling my teas in consideration of my package! I put on my best outfit, went out to meet the owner of the salon and I prepared a beautiful gift box selection of different teas and a printed package of the details of my offer. We met, we talked and he concluded by saying he was going to look into the details and contact me if he was interested in proceeding.

Weeks went by and I received no follow up. A month went by and still nothing. I decided maybe I should show more interest myself and I followed up. I dialed his number and with a hopeful voice reminded him of who I was and if he had any questions about any of my products. To make a long story short, I can't remember what his reason was, but he was not interested in proceeding. It was a no go. Not only was it a no go with the salon, but also it wasn't looking like many people were too fond of my idea of bringing quality tea to their establishments.

HOW?

As time went on I began to realize that nothing was really happening with T By Daniel. People seemed interested and I started to get a little engagement on Facebook, but other than that, there were no orders, as no tea was actually sold. A little deflated but unwilling to give up my tea dream, I continued to make videos and posts and introduce different teas to my colleagues at Yummy's. When September rolled around that year, it was a cold autumn, and if there was ever a season for tea, it was now. I visited my suppliers and I was really excited to introduce some new fall flavours like Dan's Apple Pie and Marie's Muffins and was ready to make a slam dunk this season! Just as I had guessed, people started to become more interested in these new flavours and finally, on a cool September 16, 2011, I officially sold my first packages of tea! I created the first official T By Daniel invoice for a close friend at work named Julia. There is nothing like the feeling of coming up with an idea and seeing it actually turn into something that someone else believed in.

Wow! T By Daniel actually sold something! Hope began to spark in me as a few other employees at work decided to try out T By Daniel and their family members would send them to buy more. This was all I needed to see to refuel me and mend any bit of doubt that I may of had. Week by week, I would introduce more and more new flavours based on a Facebook survey I sent out asking people to vote on what kind of flavours they would like for me to carry. I took the survey results and got to work sourcing delicious new blends that people would love. When December crept around and the Christmas holidays were upon us, people from work would approach me asking me if I had any holiday teas or gift sets because their parents or their spouses loved tea. I borrowed some more money from my parents and found a neat packaging store that carried gift baskets and unique packaging ideas for the holidays and I got busy, busy, busy. I started selling gift sets and orders began to pour in from everywhere.

Even people from my mom's work place were sending in their orders for tea. I got so many orders leading up to Christmas that my dad had to create a little space for me in the living room where I could work and keep all my orders organized. In other words, I was beginning to get in the way. My dad built me a little working desk so I would stop taking over the kitchen table. The desk was a small four-foot plank of wood that he braced to the wall and with a little office chair, it became my new office.

As the Christmas craze subsided, I managed to rack in quite the number of sales. To many what I am referring to as a lot is probably nothing, but to me it meant success. I have no shame in sharing my December T By Daniel sales, which came to just over seven hundred dollars. Now your eyebrows probably fell and you might have even rolled your eyes at the figure you probably were anticipating to hear, but the real game changer wasn't the seven hundred dollars that I made. It was the new endless possibility that had now presented itself. I thought to myself, if I can make seven hundred dollars, then what is stopping me from making seven thousand dollars? If I can make seven thousand dollars then what is stopping me from making seventy-thousand dollars? Or seven-hundred thousand dollars? I remembered a quote I read from a successful millionaire that said, "If you discover a way to make one dollar, and then repeat that process one million times, then you'll be a millionaire." Such wise words and thus I adapted this way of thinking. With my confidence now at an all time high, sales to prove my concept, and my new desk, I decided it was time for me to officially say good-bye to Werner and the Yummy's team. It wasn't easy, but by this point Werner knew I was serious about doing this tea thing, and besides my replacement manager John was in full gear. I fulfilled my last few shifts, said my farewells, munched my last pizza and I was no longer employed at Yummy's Pizza, or anywhere else for that matter. I was officially self-employed with T By Daniel.

HOW?

Still buzzing from the December gold rush, I was super motivated and pumped for the New Year! With people now purchasing my teas and my full time dedication given to building T By Daniel, I couldn't wait to see where I could take this company. Then January happened. Christmas was over, credit cards were maxed out and people were back to focusing on whatever they were focused on before September. A few orders came in during that month and a couple of my former teammates purchased some more tea, but at the end of the month, T By Daniel's future looked bleak once again. We made a whopping one hundred and fifty dollars for the entire month. I still had to contribute rent even though I lived at my parents' house; I still had to pay my car payments, my insurance and my gas. I no longer had the benefits of a supplementary income so we were now completely living off of Renata's income. And in case you were wondering, Renata wasn't making a six-figure income. Not even close. So needless to say, times got a little rocky. With February at the door and Valentine's Day right around the corner, I didn't even spend a second in doubt about January's sales, but instead kept focused on being positive about what I had to offer and started thinking about how I could grab people's attention once again.

Looking back at the early stages of T By Daniel, I'm so grateful for the January's. It was times like those that really showed me how to overcome adversities, how to pick myself back up in business and the importance of not being motivated by money. Money had proven to me that it was no different than temperature. Canadian temperature at that! At 12:00 p.m. it's super sunny and hot and by 2 p.m. it's a blizzard. Money can be up one second and down in the blink of an eye. If I focused my motivation in business based on money and it's bipolar frequencies, then I too would be up and down and this was not the way I wanted to live. Instead, I grounded myself in my purpose, which was, why am I doing what

I'm doing? What is the foundation of why I started this tea company?

When I remembered the true reason why, it pushed me to continue to roll out of bed excited to see what kind of positive impact I can leave in the world that day.

BRICKS

2012 will forever be defined as the building years of T By Daniel. Absolutely every lesson I've learned in running my own business was learned through trial and error. I get many emails from individuals who are considering starting their own business, who request to meet with me to pick my brain about the ins and outs of starting up. Occasionally I do accept the invitation and try and find time to meet the person or converse via email chats. On many of these occasions, one of the first questions the person will ask me is "how did I do it?" What were the struggles I experienced? What should they avoid? Where should they get funding? How much does this cost and how much does that cost. I'm willing to bet that 99% of the time, the ambitious individual is unsatisfied with my answers. Why, you ask? Well, I just don't believe that someone can take their exact experience, their mistakes, their victories, and their methods and lay it down for someone else as a game plan. I don't think that's fair to the person. The truth is, nobody's experience is going to be exactly like yours. The greatest advice I can offer someone who is considering starting a business is to just do it. Go out into the world and start creating your story, and this way you will learn from your own mistakes and your own successes. Some people might say, "OK so why are you writing this book with business tips and personal experiences?" Telling your story is completely different than advising someone to try to live your story. Storytelling is an effective tool that can be used to inspire people to understand that sometimes other people in the world are in the same situations as you or worse. When you hear about someone who was able to rise up out of a bitter situation or a tough time and go on to do something positive, you can take encouragement from that person's story and apply that motivation to your own. At the end of the day, your story has to be authentic to you.

Another question I often get asked is "What does your day usually look like?" They usually look at me with big dreamy eyes, awaiting the glamorous stories about being able to make my own schedule, how everyday I wake up and go to important meetings in skyscrapers, and how in my spare time I travel to exotic places…yeah, not quite. One of the most challenging things about building a business is learning how to create steady work for yourself, everyday. After all, if you're not working, as a startup, for the most part you're not making any money. I was so use to always working for someone, that when it came time for me to work for myself, I didn't even know where to start. I realized how hard the owners in the previous companies I had worked for must have worked to keep me and all their other employees' busy and employed everyday. Even in a management position, I always had work laid out for me. At a certain time I had to open the store and do paper work or file the receipts. But now I was running my own business full time, so when I wake up 7:00 a.m., what's the first thing I should do? You can only be on your computer for so long until you find yourself just creeping people's Facebook pages or find yourself reading the latest Hollywood scandal. One day I read a few articles about good productivity practices that every entrepreneur should do to create good working habits. The article was very straightforward in its methods. Create a to-do list and categorize all your tasks into groups of importance and priority. The to-do list was supposed to be categorized like this: urgent, not urgent, very important, and not very important. After my chart was created and I had my to-do list all filled out, I simply filtered through the list putting things in their right places and *voila*! My workday was created. Everyday when I woke up, I disciplined myself to spend the first fifteen minutes populating this list and soon it became a vital part to navigating the course of my day, everyday. Another very important practice I focused on was making myself accountable to someone. In most cases it was my wife, as I almost felt obligated to tell her in detail what I accomplished while she was out working and I was at home everyday. I can only imagine how upset and taken advantage of Renata would have felt if she knew that I was at home everyday doing absolutely nothing on Facebook while she's out working extra hard to make a living for us. This also inspired me and motivated me to work smarter, harder and to hustle like never before.

Now I had my time management down. I had practices in place on how to be effective and accountable, great. But how do I make a consistent income? Well, bells of gladness sounded the day I discovered what tradeshows and events were and how easy they were to get into. After researching many different ways that small businesses can promote themselves, I learned about displaying my products at tradeshows. A tradeshow is an exhibition where certain businesses in a specific industry come to display their latest products or services, either to the end consumer or sometimes business-to-business. This was like a gold mine for me. While searching out cities where I would like to try and sell our products, I came across a mom-to-mom super sale called Mama and Chicks. New moms plus tea sounded like a good idea; so I scraped together two-hundred dollars to purchase a vendor table. This was my first event and I wasn't sure what to expect

but I figured at that point I might as well try something new, especially something that would expose me to hundreds of new people, who would never hear about T By Daniel. I carried along my wife and two other friends to assist me just in case we got busy and I needed help. I had packaged a bunch of teas and printed up some business cards with the 'T' logo on them in hopes of selling some pouches and then making customers aware that I have an online store where they can purchase more tea. My team and I were all setup and ready for the event planner to open the doors for the public to come in. We couldn't see if anyone was lined up to come in or not and that's the scary part about tradeshows. You never know what you're signing up for until you're there. I weighed out all the possible outcomes in mind. Best-case scenario, people love the tea samples, they buy a few pouches and then weeks later, they place an online order for more! The worst-case scenario would be nobody showing up at the show and me being out $200. The event planner made an announcement that they were opening the doors and concluded by wishing all the vendors a successful shopping event.
And, *POW*!

The last time you probably saw that onomatopoeia was in your favorite superhero comic book when the good guy socked the villain in the face. That's exactly what the rush of moms on a mission felt like. Strollers and children and moms looking for cute products and great prices flooded the event floor in seconds. Our game plan was to let me do all the talking while everyone else pours tea samples and keeps track of which teas we were selling while collecting payments. Our plan failed immediately. In moments, our vendor booth was packed with groups of women varying in age trying samples, asking questions about tea health benefits and inquiring about prices and special offers. We were in over our heads. The biggest mistake I made was not properly training any of the helpers I had brought with me about the products we were

HOW?

selling. Renata had some form of knowledge about the teas as she was forced to learn about them through my constant bickering about tea, but as for the helpers, they were completely clueless. In this scenario, I was forced to exercise leadership and learn how to take control of a situation and get the workflow in order. I literally felt like a baby being thrown in a pool and being told to swim. Luckily within the chaos, there was a very brief break where we didn't have any moms at our booth and I decided to try and implement some structure and organization to our mini operation. It started with a sixty-second briefing on what tea we were sampling and how to highlight three main health benefits about the tea. Next I assigned one stationary person to picking the tea orders and another to cashing the customers out and tracking teas that had been sold. Renata would manage sampling and also assist customers when it was too overwhelming for me. As for me, it's show time! I remember how easily I use to grab everyone's attention when I would enter a freestyle battle back in my high school days, so I figured If I could re-direct all these shopping moms attention to me, then I could give the information about the teas once to a larger group instead of having to repeat the same spiel over and over to every mom that approached our booth. The second wave of rushing moms began to flood in and this time we were ready. I stood in front of our little booth and started calling out to women passing by, taunting them with delicious tea samples and signaling them to come and smell the amazing aromas of our teas. As they were allured over to our booth, Renata came beside me with a silver tray loaded with tea samples and as they picked the samples off the tray and began sipping away, I started giving my pitch about the benefits and tastes they could expect from the tea while simultaneously reaching for another smell sample to keep them interested. In about sixty seconds or less, the majority of our audience became fully engaged and came closer to our booth to begin shopping for tea. After we helped them pick out their favourite flavours, we brought to their attention an amazing special offer giving them five of their favourite flavours for only twenty dollars. The amount of twenty dollar bills that were thrown at us that evening made our booth look like someone planted dynamite in a bank.

The event, to say the least, was a great success! When the event ended and we finished tearing down our setup and packing everything into the car, we definitely left lighter than we came and this was good sign. After enduring an eight-hour shift, I took the crew out to Wendy's to reward them for all their hard work. (Hey, we'll get to Red Lobster one day. Give me a break!)As we packed into the car and headed back home, we dissected the entire experience, the good, the bad and the ugly and there was a lot of laughter and suggestions to go around. When the dust had settled, Renata and I got home to our bedroom and laid all the bills and change out on our bed. Once we had finished counting the money, we had a total of five hundred dollars and change. We were so excited to see that we actually profited from our first investment in an event. This was my first official return on investment.

I had tapped into something special and something that had the potential to help me grow my business, gain exposure for my brand, increase my ecommerce traffic, and most importantly interact with new people all the time. So, 2012 became the year of events and tradeshows. The Mama and Chicks Show took place early March and now the hunt for more events was on. Everything was looking up. But of course, as life would have it, what goes up, must come down (again). About two weeks after our first successful event at The Mama and Chicks Show, Renata received a letter from her workplace saying that her position with the company had been taken away due to a cut back in labour throughout the company.

"TIM-BER-RRR!" Right when things seemed to be looking up for T By Daniel, we lose our last steady flow of income. Renata's income was anchoring us, putting food on our table, keeping us clothed and enabling us to make our car payments, not to mention funding the majority of our business endeavors. Of course my parents were there for us incase things got really bad, but as a 24 year old married man, I wanted to believe that I was able to somewhat sustain myself. So, that was that and there we found ourselves both unemployed, or I guess, self-employed, and trying to build a business with absolutely no capital to our name.

As the old saying goes, when life throws you lemons, you make Gatorade...or lemonade or something like that. Of the many life lessons that my dad has taught me, I can honestly say that the one I'm about to share has had the deepest impact on me, and the way I now view circumstances in life. One night, while we were discussing all of our new challenges and roadblocks, my dad asked me, "Dan what can a slingshot teach you about business and about life?" I took a second to think about it and my face instantly transformed into the face of someone who is in a very deep thought. For some odd reason I couldn't even think of a silly answer, perhaps I was a bit lost for words due to the fact that my dad had actually constructed a real slingshot using small tree branches from outside and elastic bands. It looked like something Dennis The Menace would carry around. Anyways, after a solid minute of brain cramps, I finally gave up and replied, "Dad, I have no clue." He armed the slingshot with a crunched piece of paper or some other small object and said, "Let's say you start this T By Daniel business and everything works out smoothly. Everyone is buying your tea, you're making lots of money and every event you go to is a huge success and life is just smooth. When it is time for you to take the next step in your life and move forward, this is how far you'll go." He pulled the object that was sitting in the rubber band back less than an inch as to represent minimal setbacks. When he released the object, it basically fell right in front of him. I looked on attentively. My dad picked up the object and continued on. "Now let's say you start this T By Daniel company and things start off rocky. You have limited money in the bank, Renata loses her job, you go to an event and nobody shows up, and all these different setbacks keep happening in your business or in your life." This time he set the object in the rubber band and pulled it all the way back to represent all the many setbacks he had just mentioned. By this point I completely understood his parable and was speechless. He said, "when it's time for you to take the next step in life and move forward, this is how far you'll go." He released the rubber band sending the small object flying across the room, and then he concluded by saying, "Our setbacks in life only propel us farther ahead." Wow. My life just changed, again.

Today, years into my business, I have also become a motivational speaker and I have had the opportunity to speak and share my story to hundreds of people, students and future entrepreneurs across the country. Whether it be a grade school, a college or university, a corporate audience, a community group or youth at risk, I end my presentation with the exact same lesson my dad taught me that day. I call it the "Sling-Shot Theory." After understanding this way of thinking about setbacks, Renata and I viewed her layoff as an opportunity to push us farther ahead with T By Daniel. Renata was now home with me assisting me in finding affordable events to attend, so that T By Daniel was not sitting dormant. Two heads are a lot better than one. Kijiji became our new best friend and every day Renata and I spent hours searching for local events. We started finding all kinds of events, both big and small. Some events were held at nearby schools as a way of supporting fundraisers or year-end celebrations. There were health fairs, farmer's markets, pampering parties for women, luxury-shopping events, and we attended them all. There were a few occasions where we even setup a tea tasting station at an outdoor garage sale, similar to a

HOW?

lemonade stand. Anywhere tea could be served, we were there. It didn't matter how far the event was, it didn't matter what day or what time or for how long, we were there. Our strategy was simple. Book into events that cost very little and our goal is to make a little bit more than we spent, all while creating new customers and a T By Daniel customer database populated with emails and phone numbers. Thank God our strategy actually started working! Every event we went to we ended up leaving with more than what we had paid to be there, and a lot of new people drinking T by Daniel teas. Renata and I never sat down once at an event or a tradeshow as we quickly noticed that passing customers would walk right by our display booth if we were not standing up and ready to engage with them. It was very easy for Renata and I to stand out at events because most of the other vendors were sitting down, on their phones or chatting with their neighbouring vendors. I certainly did not pay a hefty vendor fee to come and sit down in front of a table with my name on it and cross my fingers hoping someone tries a sample or buys one of my teas. This was our life. If we didn't work it, we had nothing. By the last quarter of the year, T By Daniel had become a well-known name in the events circuit and Renata and myself had a very polished approach to tradeshows and events. Our genuine love for people, delicious teas and experienced showmanship seemed to resonate with people quite well and this was proven in the huge increase of sales T By Daniel was raking in. We had done a mini rebrand to the company, making it a little cooler and more eye-catching (as we learned from many other companies at the various shows we would attend.) That same year, we were selected as October's business of the month in our city, Brampton. The feature article and with the story of a young couple and a startup business, became a beautiful story within the Brampton business community and many organizations began to reach out to us inviting us to events to supply them with tea and also to

share our experiences of starting a business.
"To build the greatest building the world has ever seen, you must start by laying the first brick."- Anonymous.

THE BEGINNING

The end of the year was approaching, and the glory months of business were just around the corner. November was the month that held the now infamous Brampton Christmas Market and Santa Claus Parade, and this event brought thousands upon thousands of people from all over the community to celebrate the Christmas holiday season and shop cool local businesses. We were super lucky to have been selected to occupy one of the ten mini barn houses that were transformed into small local shops where a select few vendors and artisans could display their products, in hopes of selling some cool holiday gifts and stocking stuffers. Lucky for Renata and I, we just so happened to sell tea and everybody loves tea, or at least needs one, when it's minus five degrees outside. With our exposure from the innumerable amount of events we had attended over the past few months, plus our recent feature in the Business Times newspaper, T By Daniel was a hit at the market! Hundreds of people came flooding to our booth to buy tea, to try a hot tea sample and find out if there really was a Daniel behind this T By Daniel company. The feeling was surreal and neither Renata nor myself could believe what was happening. The majority of passing patrons knew my name or had heard of me before as "The Tea Guy." Due to the large amount of people in front of our little red tea barn, it was inevitable for me to start performing. I started belting out Christmas carols, dancing and twirling and attempting my best Santa Claus voice, *"Ho, Ho, Ho! Come and try our delicious teas!"* This drew an even bigger crowd and Renata didn't mind, because we were selling tea packages left, right and center. I've come to learn that wherever there is a large group of people and something buzzing, lo and behold, you shall surely find a media representative ready to get that perfect snapshot, interview or front cover pose. Our local newspaper, The Brampton Guardian had a photographer at the Brampton Christmas Market that night, and he sure got that pose from us.

The following week was a milestone in our T By Daniel adventure. I received a tweet from a customer saying " Hey Daniel, great picture on the front cover of the newspaper!" WHAT! My heart suddenly started beating extremely fast as I was instantly taken over by excitement. I replied, typing just as fast as my heart was beating. 'Which newspaper?' As I sat at the kitchen table smiling in my heart and yelling out to Renata upstairs that we made the front cover of a newspaper, my dad came through the front door also smiling with a spread open copy of the paper and right there on the front cover, a picture of me and my lovely Renata styled with the latest red and green reindeer antlers. Renata ran downstairs to see and we smiled gave my dad a high five and began to soak in the fact that several thousand copies of this newspaper had just arrived on people's doorsteps and in their mail boxes. It was unreal. That year had been quite the adventure. The following weeks after our front cover feature in the newspaper, several media channels started reaching out to us requesting to interview me to find out the story behind this new up and coming tea company. Bramptonians wanted to know who this Daniel character was and why everyone was talking about his tea. When 2013 rolled around, we no longer had to start hunting for events to attend as they actually started hunting for us. Event planners would email me everyday asking if T By Daniel would like to purchase a vendor booth at their upcoming event. When I would ask how they heard of us or how they received our contact information, majority of the time they would respond by letting me know that a friend, another vendor or a family member told them about this crazy company who dances and sings at events and is very good at drawing a crowd. So Renata and I started booking into some of the events and rocking the show as usual. January was off to a great start, but it was when we heard about the first annual Toronto Tea Festival that things started to get really exciting. It was going to be the first of what would easily become a staple annual event in Toronto, and T By Daniel had the opportunity to attend. There was only one issue, the vendor fee was a lot more expensive than what we were used to paying. To get a small 8 x 10 space, we were well up into the hundreds, a plateau that we weren't sure we were ready to explore. I battled in mind very hard with this one because on the one hand, I know Renata and I can't afford it, but on the other hand it's a tea festival and I sell tea so I can't afford to miss it either. We had been in many events, but never one that was solely focused on tea. Imagine the possibili-teas! Like most entrepreneurs, you're always faced with a tough decision. I thought about how many people could possibly attend an event like this and especially the kind of people that would attend- our target market of tea drinkers. Then I thought about our current financial situation, which was still not in a great place. With the risk of us losing a lot of money and setting ourselves back even more financially, I still decided that it would be in the business' best interest to purchase a vendor table.

Entrepreneurship is all about risk, and you don't walk into a room with soft carpets and pillows and start working on your perfect cuddly startup business. Instead, entrepreneurship is more like walking into a room filled with sharp pins and needles as you innovate some way of starting a balloon business. The risk of failure is high, but successful people find a way to figure it out.

I gathered some money together from the T By Daniel reserve, borrowed some money from my parents and signed us up for the Toronto Tea Festival.

When the tea festival came around and we had arrived at the venue, I must admit I felt a little unqualified and inferior to the other vendors that I looked around and saw. They were tea masters, certified tea sommeliers, Chinese and Japanese tea gurus, Indian tea companies with owners and representatives who actually grew up on real tea plantations, there was companies with tea infused products who already sold their products in major big box stores, and then there was Renata and me. At this point we knew quite a bit about tea, but I mean compared to these tea gurus, we were in kindergarten. As the event got underway like most events in Toronto, people flooded in like ants out of an anthill. All kinds of people began stopping at every booth to see what interesting teas they could discover. Our company has always been founded upon some very simple and basic principles. In regards to the tea, my goal was to simplify tea in so much that even kids can enjoy a cup, rather than always thinking of tea as a beverage you only go for when you're sick. I also wanted to present tea in a fashionable and fun manner, not like your old, traditional high tea. In regards to our mission and the reason why we're even selling tea, I wanted to impact people's lives in a very positive and special way. Who knows… the next person I meet may be the last person I meet or vice versa and just like I learned from the tragedy in my life, one question will remain: what did you leave behind in this world? My initial goal with T By Daniel was to leave a huge impact on people by creating unique and memorable experiences for those I come in contact with in hopes that their day and their lives might be more fulfilled. Now if this is all I have to work with, then so be it, let's do this! I approached the event with this mind frame and sure enough it worked. T By Daniel was a very popular booth at the Toronto Tea Festival, in so much that the other vendors came by our booth to introduce themselves to us and ask us how we came up with such an awesome concept. At first I was afraid that the tea industry wouldn't appreciate our non-traditional approach to tea, but it turns out that people actually loved it. With a few tea pouches left near the end of the tradeshow, we basically sold out of all our products, and it was yet another profitable experience for us.

A few weeks after the Toronto Tea Festival, I received one of the greatest emails in T By Daniel history. It was an email congratulating us on being nominated for Brampton's 2013 Young Entrepreneur Of The Year. Wow. What an honour to be counted among Brampton's top companies and entrepreneurs, especially when in our eyes we were just a small business idea working from my parents' kitchen table. As the business gala drew closer, the committee in charge of the event released the nominees and award categories via several media outlets including the local newspaper. By this point, seeing something about T By Daniel in a newspaper had become a pretty regular thing. About a week before the award night, we found out who we were up against for the 2013 Young Entrepreneur of the Year award. It was a company called Lawn Troopers, totally different from our industry, which specialized in lawn care and maintenance. I had a pretty good scope of many of the movers and shakers in Brampton, as I had become a Board Of Trade Ambassador, which had me networking and meeting all kinds of different businesses throughout the city. I was excited at the fact that I had never heard of Lawn Troopers in the past as I felt that our chances of winning were very high due to our growing popularity in

Brampton. The night of the awards arrived and Renata and I arrived to the dazzling venue, dapper as ever and feeling confident. I was seen sporting a classic black bowtie and 007 James Bond black suit while Renata had on a classy cream and navy blue blazer with stunning drop earrings. We looked a little something like Puff Daddy and J.Lo arriving at the Grammy's; only we were a few hundred million dollars less wealthier. Upon arrival, so many people came up to us congratulating us on our nomination and encouraging us that we had this award in the bag. In the back of our minds I think we believed them, but thought it appropriate to celebrate when it was all said and done. The night went on and different categories were announced, awards were given and we enjoyed intermissions with dinner and entertainment. Finally it was time for the Young Entrepreneur of The Year category and boy did nerves come bursting in. Renata and I pulled close to each other gripping hands as we sat back and watch our nomination video play. The videos were designed to give the hundreds of business owners and companies in attendance a quick glimpse into the day-to-day operations of the nominees and also to build up some anticipation for the winner. I began to reflect on how far we had come with T By Daniel, and even more so, how far I have come personally from my many wild experiences in the past. It was like a dream come true to be in this present time, alive, excited and possibly awarded 2013 Young Entrepreneur Of The Year. I clenched my jaws tightly together and looked over at my wife as the host said, "And the winner of The 2013 Young Entrepreneur Award goes to....
(a moment of silence) Lawn Troopers!"

As every one began to applaud, the music sounded to welcome the Lawn Troopers CEO up onto the stage. I clapped my hands and smiled, casually shrugging my shoulders to my wife and those around me who were certain we would have won, and I began to feel a sting in my stomach. The sting was like a sharp emptiness in my gut that wouldn't go away. I mean yes, we worked hard and we were proud to even be nominated but there was still that disappointment and that darn second place feeling that just ate me alive. I got flashbacks to that 100m sprint final race back in high school with Antonio all over again. Just like that moment the official told us runners to take our marks, the atmosphere was just as intense. It was at that moment I remembered the humbling lesson that I learned from losing that race against Antonio that day. Being humbly competitive is a good thing; it includes feelings of nervousness mixed with confidence, anxiousness and anticipation. I reminded myself that although it's important for me to always strive to win, winning is not a feeling of comfort but instead a reward of extreme effort given. Winning is not what makes you a winner, learning how to win is what makes you a winner.

That night when Renata and I got home, we talked for a bit about the award gala and what we learned from the whole experience and like always, we were able to celebrate the adventure of it all and laugh at the disappointments. Regardless of the outcome, we both went to our bed that night as winners. The next morning, I woke up with a completely different mind state. It was a determined fierceness to excel and push T By Daniel to a completely higher level than ever before. I took the loss from the night before as momentum to go further. In my eyes, there was three hundred and sixty-four days between me and another shot at winning the very same award, and the clock started now. This must have been the way Antonio felt. When you're competitive, losing builds something concrete in you, because you never want to feel that sting again. I decided, that feeling was going to intensify my approach to business and I would start thinking like a growing company rather than a small business. Small businesses sometimes get comfortable with small thinking, but it is very possible for a small business to entertain a big mentality or leave a big impact in their industry and this is the way I started to view T By Daniel.

A couple months later T By Daniel was fortunate enough to be accepted as a vendor in the Brampton Farmers' Market. Brampton Farmers' Market ranged over a period of seventeen weeks, every Saturday from 7 a.m. - 1 p.m. from the beginning of summer until Thanksgiving weekend. It was praised for being one of the best-attended Farmers' Markets in Ontario. This opportunity was huge for our young and growing tea company. Renata and myself would literally spend all week packaging teas at home just to be able to have enough inventory to get us through each Saturday market. The Brampton Farmers' Market is said to bring one hundred thousand visitors to the downtown core throughout the seventeen week period, with ninety-three percent of the visitors actually living in Brampton. Uhh, this was kind of like a big deal. Every Saturday morning Renata and I were up bright and early at 5:30 a.m. to get ready and setup our table and tent right in the center of the downtown on Main St. We were super thrilled to be positioned smack dab center of the entire market as this meant every patron would eventually have to pass by our tent as they walked through the market. From day one, T By Daniel was a hit, selling hundreds and hundreds of packaged loose leaf teas every Saturday. We kept our returning customers interested by always rolling out a new tea blend every Saturday to create some form of anticipation. We were making money and meeting tons of new people and at one point you would think it couldn't get better than this, until one day it actually did. I don't know what I was thinking when one day I decided to attend the market randomly dressed up in a complete Super Mario costume. As parents walked by our booth with their children, whether they wanted to try or sample or not, even if they hated tea, their kids wanted to meet Mario, and in most cases this resulted in a numerous amount of selfies and pictures with families. We noticed quite a drastic increase in our sales that Saturday,

HOW?

so in other words I was on to something. The following week Farmers' Market visitors were completely surprised to see a black Elvis Presley handing out tea samples in the middle of Main St. I would dance and try to strike my best Elvis pose, while talking about tea in my best Elvis accent. When visitors would purchase a package of tea that Saturday, I concluded the sale by saying, "Thank you, Thank you very much!" Sales increased once again, and I landed on the front cover of blogs, online newspapers and I was popping up on several different social media pages from people who just had to take a quick snapshot of the rare sighting.

I seemed to have unlocked a marketing secret. We didn't need to print any flyers about our teas, or pay for any newspaper ads or do any other paid form of marketing and advertising. All I had to do was slip into a costume and instantly we were able to grab people's attention and they were more than happy to start spreading the word about who we were to their own personal networks. I now call this emotional marketing. Instead of all the traditional ways of trying to entice customers to purchase our products, we learned that people don't necessarily like to be sold to. After all, everywhere you go that's all you see, people looking for new ways to take people's money. For the most part, it actually bothers most people when you're down their throat piling them up with flyers and cards and promotional material. I find that they feel much more comfortable when you just show them a good time, entertain them and leave the choice of purchasing something entirely up to them. I'm sure many Forbes 500 companies would easily argue with my approach but it was definitely working for us. I had entered into a trend that I could no longer stop because every week visitors would come down to the market anticipating what costume I might be wearing. I certainly didn't mind dressing up every Saturday, and the most rewarding sight was to see toddlers and little children begging their parents to bring them to see the tea guy. I remember a few times people told me that their best friend or their child couldn't make it to the market on a given Saturday so they asked if it would be alright if they took a picture of me to show them what or who I was dressed up as that day. It was the most amazing experience, and from a business perspective a very profitable one as well. Finally the market season had come to an end and we had left quite the mark in downtown Brampton. We refocused our attention to booking into several holiday events that year and I decided that I was going to do something a little different. Due to the amazing success we experienced at the Farmers' Market with me dressing up in costume I thought to myself, why stop there? Why fix something that's not broken? I was very comfortable wearing costumes and dressing up and it provided a great way for our business to stand out, so I decided to start attending all events dressed up in some funky, costume. I started grabbing people's attention as soon as I would walk into a venue to begin setting up my booth. At first people looked at me like I was absolutely nuts! But by the end of the event, even vendors wanted to take pictures with me. T By Daniel began to grow rapidly and after wrapping up another fiscal year and seeing a healthy 33% growth in sales, it all became clear to me. The secret to succeeding in business is found in the first two letters of business... BU. This has become my personal trademark statement that I share with others in every presentation, every article and every TV interview that I am invited to. I didn't need a business degree or to be the most seasoned business owner in the room, I didn't need to be a tea master guru or expert marketing specialist to be successful in business. All I had to be was myself. Discovering the importance, success and value of simply being yourself, in my opinion is the beginning of truly living a purposeful life.

ME

To make a long detailed story short, when 2014 rolled around and T By Daniel was nominated once again, we were awarded 2014 Young Entrepreneur Of The Year. We went on to open up our first brick and mortar tea shop right on Main St. in Downtown Brampton directly across the street from where we had first setup for the Farmer's Market. Our shop was quickly recognized for its record-breaking grand opening in Brampton with well over 300 people packing into our shop. We were featured on Global TV News Toronto with Susan Hay on a series highlighting people who are making a difference in their community. I also went on to host my own TV show on Rogers called 'Today and Tomorrow Begin With T' discussing everything related to tea. We were awarded 2014 Consumer Top Choice Award for the Best Tea Shop In Brampton. We became the first recipient in Ontario to receive The Ontario Starter Company Grant of $5,000 towards expansion for our business. We were soon after selected as the winner of the Young Entrepreneur Pitch-Off Competition from Ignite Capital receiving a $20,000 Grand Prize.

A few months later, T By Daniel was nominated for

The Best Social Media Reach in the tea industry at The World Tea Expo in California. This expo brought tea enthusiast and tea companies from all around the world to network and recognize the movers and shakers within the tea industry. Upon arriving at the World Tea Expo ceremony held on the Queen Mary ship in Long Beach, Renata and I were welcomed by many event staff and various vendors who had been following our successes through our online media channels. Among the people I shook hands with that night was Jane Pettigrew, the author of all the tea books I had studied when I first became interested in tea. Other nominees for awards that night included companies such as DAVIDSTEA and Teavana. We were nominated out of five nominees in the tea industry and although we didn't win that award, I had learned far too many times already what it meant to win, so I was very content with the entire experience and the California vacation.

Today, T By Daniel has now evolved into T By Daniel Inc., an award winning company prized for its excellent standard of customer service and our unique approach to the tea industry. T By Daniel has provided employment to over ten staff and has become a must stop destination in the city of Brampton. T By Daniel also created a new business platform for me called DanielSpeaks, which started out as a response to an overwhelming amount of requests to speak to various audiences and share my personal experiences with students, youth at risk, and really any pair of ears that are willing to listen. Our customer service at T By Daniel has impacted so many people that I currently now teach our company's customer service training as a certified course in high schools. Renata and I also went on to start a boutique marketing company called MARSketing, that is dedicated to helping startups and small to mid-sized businesses create or rejuvenate their brand. While writing this book I was also selected to be one of three Canadian

HOW?

Ambassadors for 2015 Global Entrepreneurship Week, where I travelled across three major cities in Canada to explore the different entrepreneurial ecosystems that our great country has to offer. I have personally grown a lot since the days of being a class clown, however, I haven't lost the clown in me. I'm still what I like to call the grade eight me, and I don't plan on changing that. Our company T By Daniel has grown a lot as well, and without a doubt I credit this to the fact that our motive in what we do and why we do it, is built on a solid foundation that cannot be broken. I came from a very hopeless past considering the many setbacks and dark times I've gone through, and many people would say that I am the perfect candidate for a success story. Maybe that's true, or maybe it's not, but with all these accolades that I now have under my belt, I still don't believe that these things make me successful or special, I think they just make me, me.

If people could learn to focus on who they really are inside and what they truly value rather than measuring their success on exterior things, like how much money they have or how big their companies are or what cars they drive, I think many people would come to realize that they actually have a story worth telling. As you build your story and share your story with others, you begin to impact people's lives, and once you've left a positive impact in someone's life, congratulations, you have officially become successful. Here's how I did it. First I realized that I can't do it. After that realization, I learned to put my faith in God. My faith in God kept me, my parents' advice guided me, my wife gave me balance, and the people I interact with everyday gave me a reason to continue. Life is but a series of pages that we write on every single day. As we live, think, speak and do, the pages of our lives begin to populate. Every day comes with it's ups and it's downs, successes and failures, with this reality in mind, I aim to take life one cup at a time. This simplified way of thinking helps me to be narrow eyed and focused on the things that are truly important to me; like my faith, my family, helping others, and of course tea. Although I must admit, every now and then I become a little curious to see what a Coffee By Daniel scenario would look like. New adventure perhaps? I'll tell you about it in **How 2**!

ABOUT THE AUTHOR

Daniel Lewis is the funky- bowtie wearing founder of the modern, award winning tea company T By Daniel Inc. His crazy outlook on business and his Willy Wonka inspired retail tactics have garnered him and his company nation wide recognition and many awards and honours such as 2014 Young Entrepreneur Of The Year and The 2016 Business Excellence Award for communication. Daniel's success with his retail tea brand have even landed him a new exciting title as one of 3 Global Entrepreneurship Week Ambassadors for Canada in 2015 and also paved the way for him and his wife to launch MARSketing Boutique Agency and DanielSpeaks.Ca, his official public speaking platform where he shares his story and his "outside of the box perspectives" with audiences all across North America.

STAY CONNECTED WITH DANIEL

I know I'm not the most interesting person to follow, but if for some strange reason you would like to stay connected, here's where you can find me.

For Public Speaking Bookings & Inquiries

Visit: www.DanielSpeaks.ca
Or Email: info@DanielSpeaks.ca

My Social Media Playgrounds

To stay inspired. Follow @DanielSpeaks.ca on Instagram

To laugh. Follow @TbyDaniel on Instagram | Twitter

To prove your loyalty to me forever and possibly become the best of friends (electronically.)
Follow DanielSpeaks on Facebook

Send Me A Snail Mail (Letter)

T By Daniel Inc.
46 Main St. North
Brampton, ON, Canada
L6V 1N6